BEATRIX POTTER

There is a pleasure in the pathless woods,
There is a rapture on the lonely shore,
There is society, where none intrudes,
By the deep sea and music in its roar ...

Lord Byron: *Childe Harold's Pilgrimage* C.IV, st. 178

BEATRIX POTTER

HER INNER WORLD

by

ANDREW NORMAN

PEN & SWORD HISTORY

First published in Great Britain in 2014 by
PEN & SWORD HISTORY
an imprint of
Pen & Sword Books Ltd
47 Church Street
Barnsley
South Yorkshire
S70 2AS

ISBN 978-1-78159-191-8

A CIP cataloge record for this book is
available from the British Library

Printed and bound in England by
CPI Group (UK) Ltd, Croydon, CRO 4YY

Typeset in 11/13.5 Palatino by
Concept, Huddersfield, West Yorkshire

Pen & Sword Books Ltd incorporates the imprints of Pen & Sword
Archaeology, Atlas, Aviation, Battleground, Discovery, Family History,
History, Maritime, Military, Naval, Politics, Railways, Select,
Social History, Transport, True Crime, Claymore Press, Frontline
Books, Leo Cooper, Praetorian Press, Remember When,
Seaforth Publishing and Wharncliffe.

For a complete list of Pen & Sword titles please contact
PEN & SWORD BOOKS LIMITED
47 Church Street, Barnsley, South Yorkshire, S70 2AS, England
E-mail: enquiries@pen-and-sword.co.uk
Website: www.pen-and-sword.co.uk

CONTENTS

ACKNOWLEDGEMENTS

A. K. Bell Library, Perth; Armitt Collection; Athenaeum; Birnam Institute; Blackpool Central Library; Blair Castle Archives; British Mycological Society; Chapter House Museum, Dunkeld, Perthshire; Charterhouse School, Godalming, Surrey (Archives); Children's Youth & Women's Health Service; Dunkeld Tourist Information Centre; General Assembly of Unitarian and Free Christian Churches; Geological Society, Burlington House, Picadilly, London; Harris Manchester College, Oxford; Hawkshead & District Royal British Legion; Kendal Library, Kendal, Cumbria; Kendal Record Office; Lancashire Record Office; Lincoln's Inn Library; Linnean Society of London; Magdalen College Archives, Oxford; National Media Museum, Bradford, Yorkshire; National Trust; Oxford University Archives; Perth & Kinross Council Archive, AK Bell Library, Perth; Perth Museum & Art Gallery; Royal Academy Library; Royal Agricultural College, Cirencester; Royal Botanic Gardens, Edinburgh; Royal Botanic Gardens, Kew; Royal College of Art; Royal Holloway, University of London; Royal Society Archives; Scottish Borders Council Archives; Scotsman Publications Ltd; St Mary Abbots Church Archives; Zoological Society of London.

Begona Aguirre-Hudson; David D. Arbuthnot; Gordon Baddeley; Roger Banks; Dr Judy Barbour; Frances Bellis; Geoff Brown; Julia Buckley; Gill Butterfill; Wendy Cawthorne; Sonya and Gavie Chelvanayagam; Sue Cole; Steve Connelly; Robert Cook; Robin Darwall-Smith; the Reverend John Dixon; Marjorie Donald; Stephen Farthing; Professor Sir Christopher Frayling; Jan Garden; Naomi Garnett; Howard Hague; Judith Hall; Dr Stuart Hannabuss; Graham Hardy; Joe Hodgson; Kate Holliday; Judy Taylor Hough; Marie Humphries; Bruce Jackson; Meirian Jump; Sara Kelly; Susan Killoran; Elizabeth King; Ruth

Kitchin; Dr Linda Lear; Michele Losse; Liz Hunter MacFarlane; Margaret Mardell; Tracey Melvin; Craig Nelson; Zilla Oddy; Michael Palmer; Leonie Paterson; Norman Porrett; Jennie De Protani; Cliff Reed; Tony Sharkey; Ben Sherwood; Mark Simmons; the Reverend Dr Leonard Smith; Hannah Thomas; Fiona Treffry; Dr Cornelis de Wet; Irene Whalley.

Finally, I am deeply grateful to my beloved wife Rachel for all her help and encouragement.

POTTER
FAMILY TREE
(Selected)

James Potter b1776 = Mary Moore b ?

Children:
- Mary Ann Potter
- Edmund Potter b1802 = Jessica Crompton (Jessie) b1801
- Mary Hannah Potter
- Georgina Potter
- Sydney Potter
- Constantia Jane Potter

Edmund Potter b1802 = Jessica Crompton (Jessie) b1801, children:
- Edmund Crompton Potter = Mary Anderson Potter
- Clara Potter
- Rupert Potter b1832 = Helen Leech b1839
- Walter Potter = Elizabeth Leech
- William Henry Potter
- Mary Potter = Henry Enfield Roscoe / Lucy Potter

Edmund Crompton Potter = Mary Anderson Potter, children:
- Edith Potter
- Mary Catherine Potter (Kate)
- Jessica + 3 Potter (Jessy)

Rupert Potter b1832 = Helen Leech b1839, children:
- Helen Beatrix **Potter** b1866 = William Heelis b1871
- Walter Bertram Potter b1872

Walter Potter = Elizabeth Leech, children:
- Mary Welsh Scott = Edmund Potter
- Edith Potter = Walter Gaddum / Margaret +2

Mary Lucy Potter = Henry Enfield Roscoe

LEECH
FAMILY TREE
(Selected)

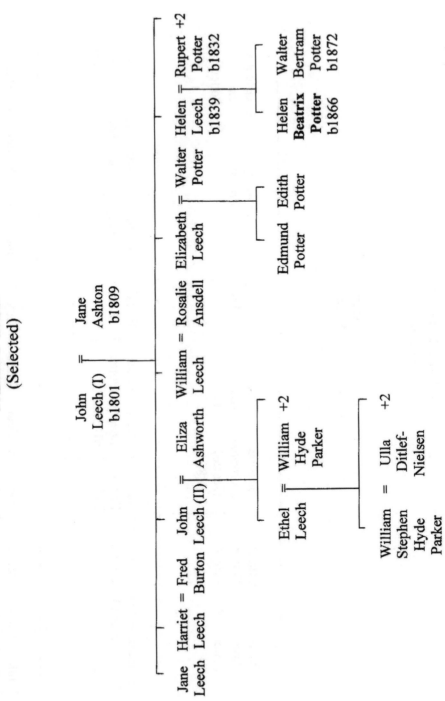

John Leech (I) b1801 = Jane Ashton b1809

- Jane Leech
- Harriet Leech = Fred Burton Leech
- John Leech (II) = Eliza Ashworth
  - Ethel Leech = William Hyde Parker +2
    - William Stephen Hyde Parker = Ulla Ditlef-Nielsen +2
- William Leech = Rosalie Ansdell
- Elizabeth Leech = Walter Potter
  - Edmund Potter
  - Edith Potter
- Helen Leech b1839 = Rupert Potter b1832 +2
  - Helen Beatrix Potter b1866
  - Walter Bertram Potter b1872

X

WARNE
FAMILY TREE
(Selected)

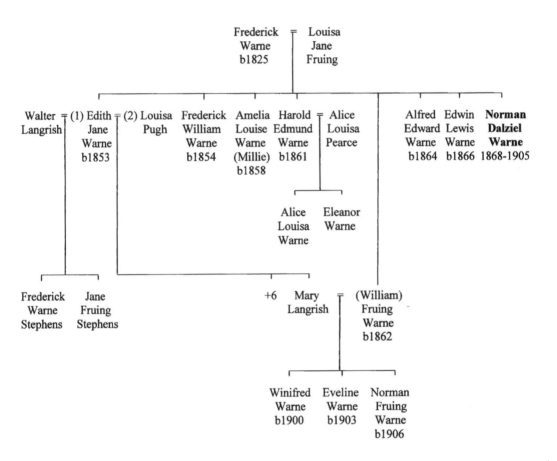

Frederick Warne b1825 ┯ Louisa Jane Fruing

Walter Langrish ┯ (1) Edith Jane Warne b1853 ┯ (2) Louisa Pugh

Frederick William Warne b1854

Amelia Louise Warne (Millie) b1858

Harold Edmund Warne b1861 ┯ Alice Louisa Pearce

Alfred Edward Warne b1864

Edwin Lewis Warne b1866

Norman Dalziel Warne 1868-1905

Alice Louisa Warne

Eleanor Warne

Frederick Warne Stephens

Jane Fruing Stephens

+6

Mary Langrish ┯ (William) Fruing Warne b1862

Winifred Warne b1900

Eveline Warne b1903

Norman Fruing Warne b1906

xi

PREFACE

EVEN PRIOR to her emergence as an infant from the crib (cot) of her nursery bedroom, Beatrix Potter was up against it for, with her prodigious memory, she could subsequently recall having been placed 'under the tyranny of a cross old nurse'.[1] This was a reference to Scottish nurse Anne MacKenzie, who introduced her to 'witches, fairies and the creed of the terrible John Calvin [French theologian and reformer]'.[2]

Many sadnesses were to follow. With no siblings of her own age, her brother Bertram, being almost six years younger, she was brought up virtually in isolation with regard to having playmates of her own age – for reasons which will later be explained. Beatrix was afflicted by two most unpleasant illnesses – one of which adversely affected her for the remainder of her life. She found herself often at odds with her mother with whom there was a clash of personalities, and hated living in London, much preferring to be in the countryside. A favourite poem of hers reads as follows:

> *As I walked by myself,*
> *And talked to myself,*
> *Myself said unto me,*
> *Look to thyself,*
> *Take care of thyself,*
> *For nobody cares for thee.*
>
> *I answered myself,*
> *And said to myself,*
> *In the self-same repartee,*
> *Look to thyself,*
> *Or not to thyself,*
> *The self-same thing will be.*[3]

This poem, which is full of poignancy and sadness, has several inner meanings. It suggests that Beatrix felt the need to be self-sufficient and self-reliant because nobody cared for her. Whether this was true or not will be discussed later. It also hints at the fact she was apt to retreat into a private world of her own.

Beatrix escaped from the pain and sorrow of the world, and from what Shakespeare referred to as 'the slings and arrows of outrageous fortune,' by creating for herself another world, one to which only she had access. The paradox was, however, that when she chose to reveal part of this private world of hers to the world at large, it resulted in her becoming, arguably, the best-known writer of illustrated children's books in the real world.

Notes

1. Beatrix to Fruing Warne, 3 January 1912. Taylor, *Beatrix Potter's Letters*, quoted in Linda Lear, *Beatrix Potter: A Life in Nature*, pp. 29–30.
2. Morse, *Beatrix Potter's Americans: Selected Letters*, p. 207.
3. This is a traditional rhyme which was a favourite of Beatrix Potter and which she used as preface to *The Fairy Caravan*. See Beatrix Potter to Mrs J. Templeman Coolidge. 30 September 1927. p. 306.

INTRODUCTION

BEATRIX Potter was born at the family home, No. 2 Bolton
Gardens, Kensington, London on 28 July 1866, which was
the twenty-ninth year of the sovereign, Queen Victoria's,
reign. This was a modern, commodious, semi-detached, terraced
house of four storeys (including basement), with seven main
bedrooms and four reception rooms, and into which the Potters
had only recently moved. No. 2 Bolton Gardens was staffed by a
butler, a cook, a housekeeper, two housemaids and a nurse;
a groom and a coachman were also in attendance. From an
upstairs window the South Kensington Museum (later, the
Victoria & Albert Museum), which had been opened in 1857
by Queen Victoria and her husband, Albert, the Prince Consort,
could clearly be seen, as a watercolour painting by Beatrix,
dated 1882, testifies. Adjacent to that building was the newly-
opened British Museum of Natural History (in the style German
Romanesque, and the size of a medieval cathedral) which was to
have important implications for Beatrix in the years to come.

The Potters were 'well to do', upper middle-class people.
Beatrix's mother, Helen, was the daughter of John Leech (I), a
Lancashire cotton magnate. Her father, Rupert, was the son of
Edmund Potter, owner of the Dinting Vale calico-printing works
in Derbyshire, the largest of its kind in the world. (Calico was a
plain, woven fabric made from unbleached cotton out of which
clothes, fabrics, and furnishings were made; coloured designs
having been printed onto it.)

Beatrix lived in an attractive part of London, where at hand were
museums and art galleries to cater for her interests in painting
and natural science. She (and her family) spent the long months
of summer and autumn in idyllic places, such as the English
Lake District (or 'Lakeland') or the Scottish Highlands, where

she was free to roam. Ostensibly, therefore, all the ingredients were present to guarantee this intelligent and creative young person, with her auburn hair and lively blue eyes, a happy childhood. Alas, life was not to be that simple.

CHAPTER 1

Beatrix's Father, Rupert

AS BEATRIX lived in a predominantly man's world, it is not surprising that men would have a major influence on her life – for better or for worse – and first and foremost of them, in her early years, was her father, Mr Rupert Potter.

Rupert Potter was born in Manchester in 1832, into a family of dedicated Unitarians (Unitarianism being a 'non-conformist' or 'dissenting' denomination).[1] Having attended local schools, Rupert entered Manchester New College in 1848. (At that time, entrance to both Oxford and Cambridge Universities was denied to dissenters, otherwise Rupert would, undoubtedly, have attended one of the Oxbridge colleges instead.) The function of the college was twofold: to prepare would-be clergymen for the dissenting ministries, and to prepare lay pupils, such as Rupert Potter, for the 'learned professions as well as for civil and commercial life'.[2] Rupert graduated from Manchester College (its degrees were awarded by the University of London) in 1851, and in January 1854 he was admitted to Lincoln's Inn (one of London's four Inns of Court).

In 1857, Rupert was called to the Bar. He subsequently practised as an equity draftsman and conveyancer, a barrister specializing in drafting complicated legal documents for the High Court of Chancery (a division of the High Court of Justice).[3]

1

Early correspondence between Beatrix and her father demonstrates the close bond which existed between them. An undated letter, sent by Beatrix from Bolton Gardens to Dalguise (the Potters' holiday retreat in Perthshire, Scotland), begins 'Dear Papa,' and ends with 'a kiss from your affectionate daughter'. It was to enquire how the dogs were; whether it was 'fine and nice', and if Mr Potter could send her a 'picture' (photograph) of anything which he found interesting.[4]

In a letter to Beatrix (again undated, but probably written in February 1874), sent to her from Dalguise, Mr Potter confesses to being 'very sleepy', having travelled there on the night train from London, and yet he takes the trouble to write to his daughter before retiring to bed. He tells her that he has made enquiries (on her behalf) from McIntosh about 'Sandy', a Scottish terrier (who was Beatrix's first dog), and relates how the Dalguise gamekeeper whistled 'and out came a brown dog with such long hair and such queer, sharp ears that I did not know him at all'. And Mr Potter's letter contained a sketch of Sandy, which he describes as 'full of fun ... [if] rather greedy, so we must teach him manners'. There were further details about Beatrix's 'pretend garden under the fir trees above the orchard', the ubiquitous roe deer which were 'very tame', and the presence of a 'little bunny' which Mr Potter had seen on the lawn. It was signed, 'I am your affectionate Papa.'[5]

In a further letter to Beatrix, written on 2 March 1874, Mr Potter states that 'Sandy' and 'Gask' (possibly another pet dog affectionately given the abbreviated name of family friend, the Reverend William Gaskell) 'are very well', that the white cat has deterred the rats and mice all through the winter, and that there are snowdrops on the lawn. 'Now if you read this letter I shall be very glad and I am my dear B. your affectionate papa.'

Mr Potter's hobby was photography (in 1869 he was elected a member of the Royal Photographic Society of London, with which he exhibited on several occasions). This is fortunate for posterity because he photographed Beatrix in a variety of poses: for example, in a group with her mother, himself, the Reverend William Gaskell, her brother Bertram and others, as they boated on Lake Windermere. One of his most charming images is of his daughter, aged fifteen, cradling her pet springer spaniel, 'Spot', in her arms. For a photograph of himself (taken, presumably, by remote control), together with Beatrix and Bertram at Lingholm(e) in the English Lake District, Beatrix made a decorative mount which she illustrated herself with depictions of wild flowers.[6] When Mr Potter acquired a new camera and handed his old one down to Beatrix, she made good use of it, for purposes which will be discussed shortly.

Mr Potter was a member of two London gentlemen's clubs: the Reform, which became a centre of liberal and progressive thought, and the Athenaeum, one of its founding members being Beatrix's favourite novelist, Sir Walter Scott.[7] Those eligible to apply for membership to the Athenaeum included:

> Gentlemen who have either published some literary or professional work or a paper in the Philosophical Transactions [of The Royal Society], or individuals known for their scientific or literary attainments, or Artists of eminence in any of the Fine Arts, and Noblemen and Gentlemen distinguished as liberal patrons of Science, Literature or the Arts.[8]

It was also stipulated that:

> bishops and judges, together with Members of both Houses of Parliament might also be admitted, whether they had published anything or not.[9]

As far as is known, Mr Potter, despite having published several important legal pamphlets, fulfilled none of these criteria and was probably admitted under 'a judicious rule that empowered the committee to bring in [admit] eminent persons by special election'.[10] Among the artists who were members and contemporaries of Mr Potter were Sir John Everett Millais, J. M. W. Turner and Sir Thomas Lawrence. No fewer than five artist members are mentioned by Beatrix in her journal, which she kept between the ages of fifteen and thirty.[11] One may therefore imagine the Athenaeum, abuzz with news that one or other of these artists is holding an exhibition at some London gallery, and Mr Potter hastening home to inform Beatrix in order that he and she, both devotees of art, may make plans to attend the function in question.

Painter Sir Charles Lock Eastlake, also a member of the Athenaeum, and his wife, Lady Elizabeth, were personal friends of the Potters, with whom they had a great deal in common. Sir Charles was, at one time, President of London's Royal Academy of Arts (1850), the first President of the Photographic Society (1853), and the first Director of the National Gallery (1855). He was also author of *Materials for a History of Oil Painting* (published in 1847, a volume with which Beatrix was doubtless familiar). Sir Charles died in 1865, the year before Beatrix was born. As for Elizabeth, she was an art critic and art historian in her own right. In her journal, Beatrix describes how she and her mother visited Elizabeth in February 1886, when the conversation was about politics, but not about art.[12]

In matters of taste Beatrix had respect for her father's judgement, both in regard to paintings, and also to sculpture. For example, when the pair went to look at the marble statue of Mr Potter's friend, the Quaker orator and Radical politician, John Bright, by Albert Joy (which had been erected in 1891 in Albert Square, Manchester), Beatrix declared, 'My father, a competent judge, considers this Statue far away the best [of that particular subject].'[13]

It is also worth mentioning, bearing in mind that both Mr Potter and Beatrix were interested in photography, that one of the most famous pioneers of photography, physicist William Henry Fox Talbot (1800–77), was a member of the Athenaeum.[14]

As one who was passionately interested in natural history, Beatrix had undoubtedly heard of English naturalist Charles Darwin (1809–82) and his book, *The Origin of Species by Means of Natural Selection or the Preservation of Favoured Races in the Struggle for Life* (published in 1859). Darwin's so-called Theory of Evolution was debated, heatedly, on 30 June 1860 at Oxford University's Museum of Natural History, the event being presided over by John Stevens Henslow, Professor of Botany at Cambridge University (where Darwin had once been his pupil).

On the one side of the debate were the Biblical Creationists led by Samuel Wilberforce, Bishop of Oxford. On the other were the Evolutionists (or Darwinians) who included biologist Thomas H. Huxley, and botanist Sir Joseph D. Hooker. Also present were Scottish lawyer and geologist Sir Charles Lyell (who found Darwin's theory difficult to accept), and zoologist and palaeontologist Sir Richard Owen (Darwin's vehement opponent). As for Henslow, he described Darwin's *Origin of Species* as a work which 'pushes *hypothesis* too far'.[15]

Interestingly, with the exception of Henslow, all these men, including Darwin himself (who had been elected in the year 1838), were members of the Athenaeum and Mr Potter would therefore have come into contact with them on a regular basis (apart from Wilberforce who had died in 1873, the year prior to Mr Potter's election to the club).

Beatrix seldom mentions Darwin in her writings but in June 1894 she does make an intriguing comment about her cousin, Mary Hutton, who she says 'seems to be curious to discover whether I should be shocked with so much [presumably talk of] Huxley and Darwin'.[16] In fact, Beatrix would not have been at all shocked, since the community of Unitarians to which she and her family belonged chose to embrace Darwin's theory rather than to oppose it, and held its creator in high regard as 'one of their own'.[17]

Beatrix was a polymath whose interests ranged far and wide. Had she been born male and come to possess the qualifications required for election to the Athenaeum, how she would have thrived amongst the intelligentsia of the land! But again, the point is an academic one, for more than a century would pass before women were admitted to the club.[18]

Notes

1. To quote from a contemporary Unitarian minister and writer:

> The oldest Unitarian movement in the world with a continuous history is Transylvania – then part of Hungary, now part of Romania.

Unitarians there look to Francis David (Ferenc Dávid 1510–79) as the founder of their Church. Reed, *Beatrix Potter's Unitarian Context*, p. 2.)

David was Bishop of Transylvania's Hungarian churches and also Court Preacher to John Sigismund, Prince of that country.

Unitarianism was a by-product of the sixteenth-century Protestant Reformation, an attempt by German religious reformer Martin Luther to reform the Roman Catholic Church. Subsequently, it was possible for the Protestant Christians of Europe to read the Bible in their own native languages. (Hitherto, Bibles had been written exclusively in Latin, a language which ordinary people could not understand.)

In 1662 the Government of England responded to the emergence of Unitarianism and other 'dissenting' faiths, such as were practised by Presbyterians, Baptists, Congregationalists, Independents, etc., by passing the Act of Uniformity. This required ministers of the Church, together with laymen and women, to accept the doctrinal and liturgical conditions laid down by the Church of England, and those who failed to do so faced penalties and persecution.

2. Davis, *A History of Manchester College*, p. 56.
3. Mr Potter's chambers were at Number 8 (from 1858 to 1861), and subsequently at Number 3 (from 1862 to 1892), New Square, Lincoln's Inn, London. Information kindly supplied by Lincoln's Inn Library.
4. Taylor, *Beatrix Potter's Letters*, p. 11.
5. Rupert Potter to Beatrix, Dalguise, ? February 1874. The Victoria & Albert Museum.
6. Collection of the Victoria & Albert Museum.
7. Founder of the Athenaeum was Anglo-Irishman John Wilson Croker (1780–1857), a classical scholar of Trinity College, Dublin who was Tory Member of Parliament and Secretary of the Admiralty. The club was established on 16 February 1824 when a committee of fourteen met, under the presidency of eminent chemist and inventor Sir Humphry Davey, President of the Royal Society. It is interesting to note that founder members of the Athenaeum included Beatrix's favourite novelist, Sir Walter Scott, and Henry Crabb Robinson, who, like Mr Potter, was a barrister by profession.

The thirty-seven existing members who were willing to 'certify his [Mr Potter's] eligibility from personal acquaintance or knowledge of his works' for the club included, not surprisingly, representatives of the legal profession including nine barristers, five Queen's Counsellors, a lawyer and the Lord High Chancellor himself! Others included Sir Henry E. Roscoe, chemist, former parliamentarian, Fellow of the Royal Society and Vice-Chancellor of London University who, as already mentioned, was Beatrix's uncle; William B. Carpenter, naturalist and physiologist who was the son of a Unitarian minister; Sir G. Osborne Morgan QC MP, a campaigner for religious equality; Sir James Caird, jute baron and philanthropist; Sir Lyon Playfair, Scottish scientist and Liberal parliamentarian; Richard Holt Hutton, author and biographer of Sir Walter Scott and Editor of the *Spectator*; and George Scharf, who was Secretary to the National Portrait Gallery. There were also two physicians, the pianist and composer Sir William Sterndale Bennett and several serving or former Liberal MPs.

8. Cowell, *The Athenaeum*, p. 11.
9. Ibid, p. 10.
10. Griffiths, *Clubs and Clubmen*.
11. Beatrix's Journal: 1881–97. For a period of fifteen years Beatrix kept a secret diary. It consisted of approximately 200,000 words and was begun in 1881 when she was aged fifteen (and possibly even prior to that, some of its pages having been destroyed). It ended some fifteen years later, on 31 January 1897, when she was aged thirty. According to author Margaret Lane, this so-called 'Journal':

> had lain undiscovered in a drawer at Castle Cottage, Sawrey [Beatrix's former home in the Lake District] until the year 1952, when Mrs Stephanie Duke [née Hyde Parker], the first cousin, [of Beatrix] once removed, who had inherited the house ... came upon the bundle in the attic. She could make nothing of it. ... when Mr [Leslie] Linder, an engineer [from Buckhurst Hill, Essex] who in middle life had made a hobby of collecting Beatrix Potter's works ... paid one of his visits to Sawrey ... [he] learnt from Mrs Duke of the existence of the code-writings, which by this time had been deposited at Hill Top in the care of the National Trust. [Lane, *The Tale of Beatrix Potter*, p. 47.]

'Code-writings' refers to the fact that the journal was written in code, and Hill Top was a farm which Beatrix subsequently came to own. Having made many attempts to break the code of Beatrix's journal, Linder finally succeeded on Easter Monday 1958. (*Journal* xxiv). He now proceeded to perform the monumental task of translating the complete work, which was published in 1966 by Frederick Warne & Co. From this document, much may be gleaned about Beatrix's daily life and private thoughts, as she passed from childhood into adulthood).

12. Linder, *The Journal of Beatrix Potter from 1881–1897*, 1 February 1886.
13. Ibid, 24 September 1895.
14. One of the two most famous pioneers of photography, physicist William Henry Fox Talbot (1800–77), was a member of the Athenaeum (the other was Frenchman Louis Daguerre). In 1841 Talbot had patented the 'calotype', the first process for producing photographic negatives from which prints could be made. However, in August 1852, *The Times* newspaper published a letter on the subject from Irish astronomer Lord Rosse, President of the

Royal Society and member and trustee of the Athenaeum, and Sir Charles Lock Eastlake. (The Potters were personal friends of the Eastlakes, Sir Charles being the author of *Materials for the History of Oil Painting*, published in 1847, a volume with which Beatrix was doubtless familiar). Rosse and Eastlake called upon Talbot to relax his enforcement of his photographic patent, on the grounds that his action was stifling the development of the science of photography.

15. *Recollections of J. Herbert*, Cambridge University: Darwin Archives.
16. Linder, op. cit., June 1894.
17. Reed, *Beatrix Potter's Unitarian Context*, p. 6. Had Beatrix been an Anglican, then she might well have been 'shocked' by Darwin and his theory. However, as one who embraced the broad principles of Unitarianism, there was no reason why this should be the case. In the words of leading contemporary Unitarian, Alan Ruston:

> Unitarianism was possibly the only church organization within the 19th-century Christian fold not blown off course by the Darwinian revolution; indeed the movement embraced the new thought, as it has, in the main, subsequent scientific advances. (Ruston, Alan. *Unitarianism: The Continuing Story*).

Or, as another leading Unitarian, the Reverend Cliff Reed stated, Unitarians 'had generally welcomed Charles Darwin's *The Origin of Species* when it was published in 1859'.

Interestingly, the Reverend Thomas R. Malthus (1766–1834), whose book *An Essay on the Principle of Population and a Summary View of the Principle of Population* (published in 1798) had inspired Darwin in the formulation of his theory, had, like Darwin, been a member of the Athenaeum.

18. Women were first admitted to the Athenaeum in 2002.

CHAPTER 2

Beatrix's Mother, Helen

A T TIMES, as is the case with most children, Beatrix found both her mother and her father irritating, but it was with her mother that she had the greater difficulty. With Mrs Potter there was a clash of temperaments; for both she and her daughter were exceptionally stubborn and determined characters, and their life together, at times, resembled a tug of war. A fundamental difference between the two was that, whereas Mrs Potter was essentially a 'town person' who travelled around in a fine carriage and enjoyed socialising, Beatrix, on the other hand, yearned to be in the countryside, and found London, where she never felt well, to be oppressive and an unhealthy place.

On 18 April 1883, for example, Beatrix recorded, 'Mamma decided on Miss A. [Annie Blanche] Carter ... Bertram going to school tomorrow.' This was a reference to the arbitrary appointment by Mrs Potter of a new governess and tutor in German for her daughter – who at the age of almost seventeen considered herself to have outgrown the need for such a person. (In fact, Beatrix was only three years younger than Annie, who was aged twenty!) This plunged Beatrix into the depths of despair. Said she, dryly, a week later:

A nice way, a lively [way], to begin with a new governess. Only a year but if it is like the last it will be a lifetime. I can't

9

settle to anything but my painting, I lost my patience over everything else. [And then, resignedly,] There is nothing to be done, I must watch things pass – Oh *Faith, Faith*.[1]

Subsequently however, Beatrix was to say that 'Miss Carter' was the governess whom she had liked the best. She was 'very good-tempered and intelligent', even though she 'had her faults ...'.[2] However, Annie remained with the Potters for a period of only just over two years. She left their employ in June 1885, and the following year married civil engineer Henry Harry Moore, and set up home with him at 20 Baskerville Road, Wandsworth. Subsequently, as will be seen, Beatrix would have cause to be extremely grateful to Annie for keeping some precious letters which she had sent to Annie's children.

Mrs Potter's stubbornness was one thing, but it was her lack of consistency that Beatrix found intolerable. On 28 March 1884, for example, when her mother's vacillations were driving her to distraction, Beatrix declared:

> Have been very unsettled this week, first Mamma said that I should go to Manchester, then that I could not, then I was to stop at home with the girls [which girls these are is not specified], then it was decided I should go to Camfield ...

'Manchester' was a reference to the home of Beatrix's late maternal grandparents, John (I) and Jane Leech (Gorse Hall, Stalybridge), John having died in 1861 before Beatrix was born and Jane only three months previously, in January 1884. Camfield was a reference to Camfield Place, Hertfordshire, the home of Beatrix's paternal grandmother, Jessica ('Jessie') Potter, whose husband, Edmund, had died in October 1883. Continued Beatrix:

> but now I am to go to Manchester tomorrow. I am afraid Grandmamma Potter will be very disappointed and I very much wished to go, but it is the last chance of seeing the old house [Gorse Hall].[3]

During her late teens and early twenties Beatrix suffered a prolonged period of intense depression, caused by her having contracted an infectious disease which went undiagnosed at the time, and has remained so ever since – until now. This disease, and its cause and effects, will be discussed shortly. In fact, this illness was followed by another – also infectious, which was ironic, in view of the fact that her mother had made strenuous efforts to protect her from such calamities. Lady Ulla Hyde Parker (née Ditlef-Nielsen, a Dane from Copenhagen) was the wife of Sir William Stephen Hyde Parker, Beatrix's cousin once removed.[4] According to Ulla, Beatrix once told her that 'when she [Beatrix] was a child she was not allowed to meet or mix with other children', because her mother, Mrs Potter, 'was so afraid we [i.e. she and her brother Bertram] would catch germs'.[5]

Mrs Potter was right to be anxious, for it should be remembered that in Victorian times diseases such as cholera, typhoid, scarlet fever, tuberculosis and measles, the latter being a far more serious disease then than it is now, were the scourge of society. Also, such diseases were indiscriminate, as far as which class of person they chose to attack, and even where Beatrix lived, in the apparently salubrious environs of Bolton Gardens, there were many ever-present hazards to health. On 31 October 1882, for example, Beatrix reported in her journal that their neighbours, the Wicksteeds, had scarlet fever. In the spring of 1884 she reported, 'Smallpox very bad in London'. Even more alarmingly, on 5 May 1884, she noted that there was 'smallpox next door'.[6] A fortnight later she complained that her neighbours 'are exceedingly careless and have never told us it was in the house'.[7]

To be fair to Mrs Potter, unlike Beatrix she did not leave any records behind of her thoughts and feelings and therefore one is dependant upon the words of others to represent her point of view. However, what is certain is that Mrs Potter's protective (some would say over-protective) attitude towards her daughter had the effect of condemning Beatrix to live in an adult world, devoid of playmates of her own age. This effectively robbed Beatrix of a vitally important portion of her childhood, and the adverse effects of this on her future life were, as will be seen, both profound and long-lasting. At least, this is the commonly held view. But whether it is the truth or not will be debated shortly.

On the positive side, Beatrix did have free rein in other respects. When in London she did as she pleased (except for the times when she was having lessons from her governess), and when on holiday she was allowed to roam the beautiful countryside of Scotland and the Lake District as she pursued her various hobbies. Not only that, but on 18 June 1885, the Potters threw a party for Beatrix to celebrate the fact that she would shortly be coming of age. (The party was held early, because on 28 July, when Beatrix would attain the age of nineteen, the family would be on holiday in Keswick.) Beatrix said that the party, which was attended by about a hundred people, was 'the first since ten years, and for my part may it suffice for ten more ... [nevertheless] I enjoyed myself and, contrary to my own and parents' expectations, behaved well ...'.[8] Here is an indication that perhaps Beatrix was not overly enthusiastic about entering into large social gatherings. She also describes going swimming,[9] and receiving very occasional visits from Edith, Mary Catherine ('Kate'), and Jessica ('Jessy'), the daughters of Mr Potter's eldest brother, Edmund and his wife, Mary, and visiting the studio of artist Mr Brett, who is noted for his seascapes, in company with her father and with 'Kate and Maggy [presumably Margaret Roscoe]'.[10] Also, Beatrix was permitted to keep a large menagerie of pets, which were clearly a delight to her, but nothing could compensate for the absence of other children with whom to laugh, play, have fun, and generally interact, or so conventional wisdom has it.

Notes

1. Linder, *The Journal of Beatrix Potter from 1881–1897*, p. 38.
2. Ibid, 10 July 1885.
3. Ibid, 28 March 1884.
4. Sir William Stephen Hyde Parker, grandson of Beatrix's uncle, John Leech (II), and his wife Elisa, née Ashworth.
5. Linder, op. cit., 18 July 1885.

6. Ibid, 21 June 1883.
7. Ibid, 9 February 1884.
8. Hyde Parker, *Cousin Beatie: a Memory of Beatrix Potter*, p. 34.
9. Linder, op. cit., 31 October 1882, 5 May 1884.
10. Ibid, 5 May 1884, 19 May 1884.

CHAPTER 3

Beatrix's Brother, Bertram

BEATRIX'S brother, (Walter) Bertram Potter, was born on 14 March 1872, by which time Beatrix was almost six years old. Like Beatrix he received his early education at home. However, in Victorian England, whereas middle-class daughters were generally expected to remain at home and be taught by a governess, for sons it was different. They were sent away to school in early teenage life, prior to joining the family business, entering a military college, or attending university where they would be trained as teachers, doctors, lawyers, or for some other profession; and, in this, Bertram was no exception.

A week after Bertram's eleventh birthday, 21 March 1883, Beatrix, then aged sixteen, recorded that he had received his last Latin lesson from his tutor, Mr Stocker.[1] Almost a year later, on 2 February 1884, the Potters visited Eastbourne on the Sussex coast, where Bertram was to commence his schooling at The Grange, the headmaster of which was the poet Frederick Hollins. Beatrix recorded that her parents had returned to Eastbourne on 28 June to visit Bertram who was 'top of Third Class'. She then made the following, somewhat curious, comment:

> I wonder how he will turn out? Sometimes I am hopeful, sometimes I am feared ... The best upbringing has some-times failed in this family, and I am afraid that Bertram

has *it* in him. Heaven grant it is not so, but I am afraid sometimes.[2]

What the 'it' was, Beatrix did not specify, but she undoubtedly had certain misgivings about her brother.

Like Beatrix, Bertram enjoyed the outdoor life, and like her, he was particularly interested in wildlife. She recorded that he returned to school on 16 September 1884, 'leaving me the responsibility of a precious bat. It is a charming little creature . . .'.[3] Bertram, like Beatrix, also enjoyed drawing and painting. His works, which mainly reflected his interest in natural history, included depictions of a stag, a lapwing, two hares, a seal, and sweet pea blossom. He had also made a still-life study of a human skull, together with a fish and a snake, the latter two each kept in a jar of preservative,[4] and a study of ducks near a river-bank (his first introduction to ducks probably being when he sailed his toy boat on Kensington Gardens' round pond, which was a mere mile away from Bolton Gardens). Other sketches included a rugged landscape strewn with boulders at Newlands near Keswick in the English Lake District. Bertram (and his sister) even took the trouble to collect dead creatures in order to study their skeletons:

> If the dead specimen was not past skinning, they skinned it; if it was, they busily boiled it and kept the bones.[5]

Beatrix and her parents travelled to Eastbourne to visit Bertram once more on 8 November, having been informed by his school that his 'conduct [and] work [were] very good'.[6] Bertram's final term at The Grange ended on 29 July 1886.[7] That September he commenced at Charterhouse, the public school in Godalming, Surrey, as a boarder in the Upper Fourth Form (the top stream); the name of his house being 'Hodgsonites'. (In Britain private schools are traditionally called 'public schools'.) Why Charterhouse? A likely explanation comes from writer Vere H. Collins:

> Contrary to the usual idea of the English Public School, Charterhouse, though the main interest was [competitive]

games, was very tolerant to unconventional boys. Of course, they did not enjoy popularity, but they were left alone unless they were aggressive.[8]

Bertram's time there, however, was to be brief, for at the beginning of the following April, as Beatrix recorded in her journal, he became unwell.

Bertram taken ill with pleurisy at Charterhouse [and then, enigmatically] of which it is useless to speak more, for the thing is done and can never be undone.[9]

(This curious comment will be discussed later.) Fortunately, this was not a severe attack of pleurisy, and it 'mended quickly'. However, the Potters made the decision to withdraw Bertram from the school. And when, at the end of that Easter holiday, the matron who had nursed him died, tragically, from diphtheria (a common disease in those times), Mr Potter said he was 'most thankful' that he had returned Bertram to The Grange. Beatrix, echoing his sentiments, declared, again enigmatically, 'So am I for all reasons.'

Why was Beatrix so secretive about this episode, and why did she hint that there was more to it than met the eye? Years later, the probable answer would become apparent.

Notes
1. Linder, *The Journal of Beatrix Potter from 1881–1897*, 21 March 1883.
2. Ibid, 28 June 1884.
3. Ibid, 16 September 1884.
4. Collection of the Victoria & Albert Museum.
5. Lane, *The Tale of Beatrix Potter*, p. 33.
6. Linder, op. cit.
7. Ibid, December 1886.
8. Collins, *Talks with Thomas Hardy at Max Gate*, p. 32.
9. Linder, op. cit., 1 April 1887.

CHAPTER 4

Home Tuition:
Sir Walter Scott:
Beatrix's Nature

B EATRIX was taught, first by a nurse, and later by various governesses. She was fortunate, when it came to study, firstly that books (and nature) gave her particular pleasure,[1] and secondly, that she possessed a retentive memory. She wrote:

> I can remember quite plainly [from] the age of one and two years old; not only facts, like learning to walk, but places and sentiments – the way things impressed a very young child.[2]

As 'a very small child unable to read', said Beatrix, she was given a copy of *The Lady of the Lake* by Scottish novelist and poet, Sir Walter Scott (1771–1832).[3] And by the time she was aged about seven, she had 'learnt nearly all' of that poem 'by heart'.[4] She also described how she 'spent a good deal of my childhood in the Highlands of Scotland, with a Highland nurse-girl'[5], a reference to Nurse Anne Mackenzie from Inverness. And one may imagine Anne, reading aloud Scott's works to Beatrix in an authentic Highland accent, of which the great Scottish author would definitely have approved!

Beatrix gave Scott credit for the fact that she 'learned to read on the Waverley novels' (which were published anonymously by Scott under the pseudonym 'Author of Waverley', and almost entirely rooted in Scottish history). 'All at once,' she said, 'I began to READ (missing the long words, of course)', and years later she declared, 'Those great books keep their freshness and charm still.'[6] In fact, the Potters possessed the 'Abbotsford Edition' of the *Waverley Novels*, in twelve volumes, which had formerly belonged to Beatrix's grandfather, Edmund Potter.[7] Beatrix herself possessed three volumes (of twelve) of Scott's *Tales of a Grandfather* which were inscribed to 'Helen Beatrix Potter with Grandma [Jane] Leech's love 1883'.

There are many reasons why Scott and his works would have been an attractive proposition for Beatrix, the most notable one being the author's love of his native land, a love which she came to share with him.[8] He was also an advocate of social justice, tolerance, and support for the oppressed.

Beatrix's collection of books grew to a considerable size and consisted of volumes given to her as birthday and Christmas presents by family and friends, together with others handed down through the family. In 1876, when she was approaching her tenth birthday, Professor Wilson, a friend of her father, gave her a copy of *Alice's Adventures in Wonderland* by Lewis Carroll (whose real name was Charles Lutwidge Dodgson and who was an Oxford don).[9] Said Beatrix, 'I became immediately ... absorbed with Tenniel's illustrations', a reference to cartoonist and illustrator Sir John Tenniel.

'Nature' was, as already mentioned, another of Beatrix's great loves, and so it follows that books on natural history would also feature in her collection. As she recalled:

> I remember so clearly ... the morning I was 10 years old and my father gave me Mrs [Jemima Wedderburn] Blackburn's book of birds, drawn from nature for my birthday present. I remember the dancing expectation and knocking at their

bedroom door, it was a Sunday morning, before breakfast. I kept it in the drawing room cupboard only to be taken out after I had washed my grimy little hands ... The book was bound in scarlet with a gilt edge. I danced about the house with pride ... [10]

(Jemima Blackburn's book was entitled *Birds Drawn from Nature*, and Beatrix was subsequently to meet its author in London in June 1891.)

Works by American writers were also popular with Beatrix, *Uncle Tom's Cabin* by Harriet E. Beecher Stowe being another volume which was read to her by her nurse when she was 'a small child'.[11] *Uncle Remus and his Songs and Sayings* by Joel Chandler Harris was read to her, entertainingly, by family friend John Bright.[12] In *The Wide, Wide World* by American Elizabeth Wetherell (real name Susan Bogert Warner), the heroine, Ellen, is invited by her Aunt Fortune's farm manager to accompany him when he goes to feed the sheep. The part of the book which dealt with 'farm life', said Beatrix, was that which she enjoyed the most.[13] This begs the question: was it *The Wide, Wide World* which first sowed the seed in Beatrix's mind of becoming a farmer, which she subsequently did?

There is no question that, at Bolton Gardens, Beatrix received an excellent education. Furthermore, the fact that she was never sent to school was entirely to her liking. However, there was another side to the coin. As a child, Beatrix was brought up virtually in isolation from other children. This is not to say that the Potters excluded Beatrix from their own social life. On the contrary, they included her, in March 1885, when she and they went *en famille* (together with Edith, daughter of her father's brother William) to London's Globe theatre to see *The Private Secretary*, a farce by Sir Charles Henry Hawtrey. This, Beatrix described as, 'exceedingly amusing, if one could only have it without the vulgar stammering'.[14] And she invariably accompanied them when they visited the 'Grandmammas': Jessie (née Crompton), widow of Mr Potter's father, Edmund (who died in 1883), and Jane (née Ashton), widow of Mrs Potter's father, John

Leech (I, who died in 1861), with all of whom Beatrix had loving relationships. However, when Beatrix was in the company of adult relations and friends and acquaintances of her parents, she was expected to be dressed up to the nines, and to behave in a suitably grown-up manner.

* * *

It has been hitherto widely assumed that Beatrix resented not having friends of her own age to play with, was lonely on this account, and blamed her parents for being overly protective. Also, much has been made of the fact that she kept a journal, and it has been implied that her writing served as a catharsis for the pent-up frustration which she felt as a result of having such rigid and controlling parents. In it she could express herself freely and thereby maintain the integrity of her own persona. And by encoding her writings she was able to keep them secret from Mrs Potter's prying eyes. This was not only an act of covert rebellion, but also one of self-preservation. However, apart from a few minor irritations expressed by Beatrix, mainly against her mother, there is little in the journal to which her parents would have had reason to object. And there is little evidence in it to suggest that Beatrix suffered from loneliness. This then begs the question: was it from Beatrix's *own volition* that she chose to live a solitary lifestyle, at least as far as her peers were concerned?

An 'introvert' is 'a person predominantly concerned with their own feelings, rather than with external things; a shy, inwardly thoughtful person' whereas an 'extrovert' is 'predominantly concerned with external things or objective considerations; an outgoing or sociable person'.[17] From what has been observed of Beatrix's life so far, she possessed qualities of both the typical introvert and the typical extrovert. She *was* concerned 'with external things', such as the flora and fauna of the natural world, and *can* be described as 'an outgoing person' as she enjoyed visiting art galleries and roaming around the countryside. But what *is* clear is that throughout her childhood, Beatrix, as far as her feelings were concerned, behaved like an introvert. This

20

demonstrates the problems encountered when attempts are made to give people 'labels'.

Was the introverted aspect of Beatrix's character the result of 'nature', i.e. her own basic genetic constitution, or of 'nurture', i.e. the way her parents had brought her up? And if Beatrix's introverted behaviour was the result of nurture, then had circumstances been different, would she have been a more 'sociable person'? This can only be answered by observing whether or not Beatrix's behaviour changed, once the influence of her parents was removed.

Notes

1. 'Roots' of The Peter Rabbit Tales, Essay by Beatrix Potter. Published in *The Horn Book* of May 1929 in Morse, *Beatrix Potter's Americans: Selected Letters*, appendix, p. 209.
2. Ibid, pp. 207–9.
3. Linder, *The Journal of Beatrix Potter from 1881–1897*, 12 October 1892. Born in Edinburgh in 1771, Scott was descended from yeomen farmers who inhabited the Scottish Border country. His father, Walter, was a solicitor, and his mother Anne, the daughter of an Edinburgh University professor of physiology. Having embarked upon a career in law, his hobby was to immerse himself in the history and folklore of his native land, and to this end he visited the sites of the battles which the Scots had fought against the English, including the most brutal and decisive of them all, Flodden, in the year 1513. Finally, his narrative poem, *The Lay of the Last Minstrel*, published in 1805, set him on the road to becoming a poet and writer.
4. Beatrix to Marian Frazer Harris Perry, 4 October 1934. Taylor, *Beatrix Potter's Letters*, p. 365.
5. 'Roots' of The Peter Rabbit Tales, Essay by Beatrix Potter. Published in *The Horn Book* of May 1929, in Morse, *Beatrix Potter's Americans: Selected Letters*, pp. 207–9.
6. Ibid.
7. Abbotsford, after which the edition was named, was a converted farmhouse situated on the banks of the River Tweed, which was Scott's home from 1811.
8. Scott wrote a total of twenty-seven historical novels, many of them set in his native Scotland.
9. John Charles Wilson was a barrister who had been a contemporary of Beatrix's father, Rupert, at Lincoln's Inn in 1856. He subsequently lectured in law at Keble College and Wadham College, Oxford. Information kindly supplied by Oxford University Archives, Bodleian Library, Oxford.

10. Linder, op. cit., 9 June 1891.
11. Beatrix to Marian F. H. Perry, 30 March 1939. Taylor, *Beatrix Potter's Letters*, p. 400.
12. Linder, op. cit., 16 September 1884.
13. Beatrix to Helen D. Fish, 8 December 1934. In Morse, *Beatrix Potter's Americans: Selected Letters*, p. 60.
14. Linder, op. cit., 18 March 1885.
15. Pillai, 'Importance of Play in Early Childhood', www.buzzle.com. 17 September 2009.
16. Yu, Jeong, Jin, Karen Hoffman Tepper, and Stephen T. Russell. 'Peer Relationships and Friendship', www.cals-cf.calsnet.arizona.edu, 31 May 2009.
17. Soames, Catherine, and Angus Stevenson (editors), *Oxford Dictionary of English*, 2006.

CHAPTER 5

Art: A Suitable Pursuit
for a Woman

ART WAS a subject very close to Beatrix's heart, and Mr
Potter positively encouraged her in this by arranging for
her to have lessons in painting and drawing – this being
a pastime which women could indulge in on the same basis as
men. She had, she declared, an:

> irresistible desire to copy any beautiful object which strikes
> the eye ... I must draw, however poor the result, and when
> I have a bad time come over me it is a stronger desire
> than ever ...[1]

In fact, the Potters were a family of artists. Mr Potter himself, as a
twenty-one-year-old, is known to have possessed a sketchbook,
which was inscribed with the date 'Sep 1 1853'. One of his
sketches is of four dogs of various breeds, and a number of
his depictions of animals and birds were transfer-printed onto
sets of ceramic plates. In another of his sketches, he depicts what
appears to be an elderly and unsuspecting gnome asleep under a
tree as a big cat sits upon the branch above waiting to pounce
on him. In another, ducks are shown flying over a lake, the male

wearing a hat and neckerchief and the female wearing a bonnet. Such whimsical creations, which could only have been produced by someone with a highly developed imagination and sense of humour, are reminiscent of those by caricaturist, book illustrator and watercolour painter Richard Doyle (1824–83), illustrator of *Punch* magazine, who was a favourite of Beatrix. 'I have always from a little child had a great admiration for his [Doyle's] drawings in the old Punches ... [i.e. *Punch* magazines].'[2] As for Mrs Potter, she was an accomplished painter in watercolours. For example, her work 'Newton, viewed from the tower of Gorse Hall, Stalybridge, Cheshire', the home of her parents John (I) and Jane Leech, is a charming landscape in sepia with trees, a horseman and railway wagons, which served the nearby stone quarry.[3]

As for other members of Beatrix's family, Mr Potter's father, Edmund, had been a great art collector and had helped to establish the Manchester School of Design (subsequently the Manchester School of Art, of which he became President from 1855–58). Also, Mrs Potter's elder brother, William, was married to Rosalie, daughter of Sir Richard Ansdell, RA, of Moy, Inverness, who was an artist of some distinction. In fact, Beatrix mentioned his painting entitled *Returning from the Fair in Seville* in her journal, saying 'I wonder how many times he will paint that old white billy-goat.'[4] (Ansdell was noted for his depictions of animals, in particular dogs, and also of sporting scenes.)

As for Beatrix, when she was aged about six, her nurse, Anne Mackenzie, was succeeded by 'Florrie' Hammond, who was to be her governess for a period of eleven years. The two developed an excellent rapport and it was Florrie who recommended to to be the Potters that they engage an art teacher for Beatrix.[5] Two of Beatrix's early sketchbooks survive. The first, created when she was aged eight and made out of scrap paper and spare sheets of writing paper, is inscribed 'Dalguise 1875'. The second dates from the following year.

Using the knowledge that she had gained from her studies of natural history, Beatrix created images in her sketchbooks of those varieties of flora and fauna that interested her (and often, before signing the work, methodically recorded, beside each painting or sketch, the name of the species or specimen, the date, and the location where it was found). Examples were: a watercolour portrait of caterpillars crawling up the stems and across the leaves of a plant; a narcissus; harebells; orchids; marguerites, and birds' eggs. It is true to say that there was scarcely a branch of British natural history which did not attract Beatrix's attention, and no creature, however humble or outwardly unattractive, could be certain to avoid finding its way into her sketchbook. As for human beings, however, as she herself acknowledged, she had difficulty in sketching the human form. Bertram, on the other hand, at the age of only eight or nine, made some quite presentable representations in his sketchbook of both his sister and his mother.

The earliest of Beatrix's surviving drawings demonstrate not only artistic competence, but also attention to detail, as in her depiction of foxgloves and a periwinkle plant, drawn when she was aged ten, and huts on the side of a hill, with trees, steps and a stone wall, when she was aged eleven. She once said:

> I do not remember a time when I did not try to invent pictures and make for myself a fairyland amongst the wild flowers, the animals, fungi, mosses, woods and streams, all the thousand objects of the countryside – that pleasant, unchanging world of realism and romance, which in our northern clime, is stiffened by hard weather, a tough ancestry and the strength that comes from the hills.[6]

These words (which derive from the 1662 Prayer Book 'In his hands are all the corners of the earth, and the strength of the hills is his also') were written by Beatrix in the year 1940, by which time she had long since relocated from London to the North of England. Here again, Beatrix demonstrated her ability to transfer easily, from the real world into the private world of her imagination.

Like Bertram she also painted landscapes, including the valley of the River Tweed and a beech wood near Inver, both in Scotland, and gardens, including the one at 'Lakefield' house,

Sawrey (in the English Lake District, one of the Potters' favourite holiday retreats), and the village of Sawrey in the snow.

Beatrix's drawing lessons commenced in November 1878 when she was aged twelve and continued until May 1883, when she was sixteen. They were given by a Miss Cameron of whom Beatrix said:

> I have great reason to be grateful to her, though we were not on particularly good terms for the last good while. I have learnt from her freehand, model, geometry, perspective and a little water-colour flower painting.[7]

Meanwhile, in February 1880, when she was aged fourteen, Beatrix took an examination in 'freehand' and 'model', conducted by the Science and Art Department of the Committee of Council of Education at the National Art Training School, Exhibition Road, South Kensington, for which she was awarded the grade 'Excellent'. In May 1881 she took a second examination, this time in 'geometry' and 'perspective', and was awarded the same high grade.[8]

In June 1882, the year after she gained her Art Student's Certificate, Beatrix indicated that already she had become a discerning art critic, and one who did not mince her words! For example, of Scottish painter John Pettie's *Monmouth's Interview with James II*, she declared that this was a 'most unpleasant subject, beautifully painted, especially the floor'. Of English painters she was of the opinion that they 'seem to spend all their time on principal figure, and leave the background light and soapy'. Her comments are not only confined to paintings. For example, of Sir Joseph Edgar Boehm's sculpture *John, Lord Lawrence*, she said, 'Considering Mr. Boehm's reputation, his sculpture is shocking.'[9]

Beatrix revealed how, accompanied by her father, or by her governess Miss Annie Carter, she regularly visited various art exhibitions, especially those held in and around the capital. About them she made copious notes running into several pages, where each painting was analyzed in great detail:

Gainsborough's colour is very fine, but almost unnatural. He sees it so well that it makes him sacrifice the softness and shadows which are the chief charm in Reynolds's pictures, and his drawing is decidedly inferior.[10]

This was said after having visited the Winter Exhibition of Old Masters at the Royal Academy in January 1883, where she also saw three works by J. M. W. Turner which she dismissed as being '... nothing particular'. As for the four Rembrandts, had Beatrix not known that they were by the artist, she 'should not have looked at them with much interest'. However, she was 'surprised and pleased' by the Dutch landscape painters where 'Every thing was calm and smooth like the scenery of Holland herself.'[11] (Incidentally, of the great many painters and sculptors whom Beatrix mentions in her journal, fewer than sixteen were members of her father's club, the Athenaeum.)

On 21 November 1883 Beatrix recorded that the following day she was to begin a course of twelve lessons from a 'Mrs A' [unidentified]. However, a fortnight later she wrote defiantly, with reference to her painting and the priming of her canvas, 'Am using my own paints and medium, and Rowney's rough canvas ... [a reference to George Rowney & Co., art suppliers of London.] I shall not let it be in the least influenced by Mrs A ...'[12]

It was obvious from her diary entry of the 29th that the strong-willed Beatrix was at odds with Miss Cameron:

Things are going on worse. [I] Do not like my drawing lessons. She speaks of nothing but smoothness, softness, breaking the colours, and the lightness of the shadows, till there is nothing left.[13]

Beatrix had a great advantage, as far as her development as an artist was concerned, in that she was brought up in London where there were literally scores of art galleries, museums, and exhibitions on hand, featuring the foremost painters of the day. She was also fortunate in that her father shared her passion for art, and was therefore always willing to accompany her and help her to develop her critical faculties.

In March 1884 Beatrix was sad to see art works which had belonged to her late Uncle Edmund Crompton Potter, who had died the previous year, being sold by auctioneers Christie, Manson & Woods. 'The dispersal of this fine collection,' she said was 'a terrible business.'[14] In November she declared, 'I think Turner is the greatest landscape painter that ever has lived, far superior to Claude [French landscape painter Claude Lorraine] or the Dutch painters.'[15]

Beatrix not only studied paintings, but she also studied the lives of the painters in books, such as Ruskin's *Modern Painters*, purchased for her at a secondhand bookseller's by her father. In November 1883 she was to be found reading *Five Great Painters* (Leonardo da Vinci, Michelangelo, Titian, Raphael, and Dürer) by Lady Eastlake. Said Beatrix, 'On the same day Papa took me to Dover Street for [i.e. to purchase] my paints and box.'[16]

Much has been made of how artists of the Victorian era created paintings which reflected the great unanswered questions of the day, such as that of creation, the meaning of life, and the place of religion and its validity. However, whatever Beatrix's private thoughts on these matters may have been, she preferred to keep them to herself, and the opinions expressed by her in her journal address only the subject matter of the painting, the technique used by the artist, and his or her use of colour, ability to portray light and shade, etc. rather than profounder questions of what message the artist is attempting to convey. However, on viewing two pictures by Raphael, one of which was entitled *Virgin and Child* she was moved to say, 'I cannot imagine how these two pictures could be surpassed.'[17]

From Beatrix's accounts of the various exhibitions which she visited, it is apparent that women artists were seldom represented at these exhibitions. She did, however, mention the Swiss painter Angelica Kauffmann and British painter Blanche Jenkins.[18] Of Jenkins's *The First Kiss*, exhibited at the Royal Academy in June 1882, she said 'Pretty picture, particularly the little girl. Holly rather queer.' She was more enthusiastic about

Kauffmann's *Design*, which was exhibited at the Royal Academy's Winter Exhibition of Old Masters in January 1883, of which she says proudly, 'That picture ... is something, it shows what a woman has done.'

Had Beatrix wished to pursue a career in art, as her brother did, then this might have been possible. But such an occupation would have been regarded, for a woman, as being somewhat unusual. But had she achieved the required standard, would membership of the Royal Academy have been open to her? The answer is no, for apart from Angelica Kaufmann (born 1741) and English painter Mary Moser (born 1744), who were two of its founder members, no more women were elected to the Academy until Laura Knight in 1936.

The question, however, is of only academic interest for Beatrix's thoughts were heading in another direction, where art would play an important, but subsidiary, part in the proceedings. She was to become an amateur mycologist, during the course of which she would knock on the proverbial doors of another male-dominated 'Establishment', in the hope of being allowed in.

Notes
1. Linder, *The Journal of Beatrix Potter from 1881–1897*, 4 October 1884.
2. Ibid, 8 December 1883.
3. Collection of Victoria & Albert Museum. Mrs Potter was also a collector of paintings. Beatrix's brother Bertram became a professional artist, as will be seen.
4. Linder, op. cit., 10 June 1882.
5. Whalley, Joyce, Irene, Beatrix Potter Society Studies. 1999, pp. 74–5. In later years, when Florrie became old and ill with rheumatism, Beatrix kindly offered to give the former's hard-pressed nurse a holiday in her home, in order that she might rest and recuperate. Beatrix to Millie Warne, 30 September 1906. Taylor, *Beatrix Potter's Letters*, p. 146.
6. Beatrix to Bertha Mahony Miller. 25 November 1940. In Morse, *Beatrix Potter's Americans: Selected Letters*, p. 146.
7. Linder, op. cit., 28 May 1883.
8. Information kindly supplied by Professor Sir Christopher Frayling, Rector, Royal College of Art, Kensington Gore, London.
9. Linder, op. cit., 10 June 1882.

10. Ibid, 13 January 1883.
11. Ibid.
12. Ibid, 5 December 1883.
13. Ibid, 29 November 1883.
14. Ibid, 19 March 1884.
15. Ibid, 15 November 1884.
16. Ibid, 22 November 1883.
17. Ibid, 29 August 1883.
18. Ibid, 10 June 1882, 13 January 1883.

CHAPTER 6

The Reverend
William Gaskell

AS A CHILD who, for whatever reason, was virtually devoid of childhood friends, Beatrix found herself living in a predominantly adult world, and one of several adults with whom she established a friendly rapport was the Reverend William Gaskell.

From 1828 until the end of his working life Gaskell had served as Minister at Cross Street Chapel, Manchester's principal Unitarian place of worship, which was also that of the Potter family. In addition he served from 1840 as Secretary to Manchester New College and in 1846 became its Professor of History, Literature and Logic. It was Gaskell who had tutored Mr Potter at Manchester New College, since when the two had become lifelong friends. In 1854 he co-founded the Unitarian Home Missionary Board.

The humane, compassionate, and energetic Gaskell strove to relieve poverty and to improve the living conditions of the poor at a time when Manchester contained some of the worst slums in England. This involved promoting measures which would reduce the transmission of diseases – in particular, cholera and typhus.

31

He also strove to provide schools, libraries, training facilities, and soup kitchens for the working classes.

Gaskell's wife was the novelist and biographer Elizabeth Cleghorn Gaskell (née Stevenson), who died in 1865, the year before Beatrix was born. Her views were entirely in accord with those of her husband, and this is evident in her novels where she sympathizes with Manchester's working-class poor and challenges the 'hypocrisy' of so-called 'Victorian values'.[1]

As for Unitarians,

> they believe that freedom from prescribed creeds, dogma and confessions of faith is necessary if people are to seek and find truth for themselves. Shared values and a shared religious approach are a surer basis for unity than theological propositions. Because no human being and no human institution can have a monopoly of truth, it is safer to admit that from the outset. [The Unitarian community is] A community of the spirit that cherishes reason and acknowledges honest doubt; a community where the only theological test is that required by one's own conscience. Above all, Unitarians are bound by a sense of common humanity.[2]

Finally, Unitarians, who regard both the Bible and the Church as fallible, believe that for every individual the seat of religious authority lies 'within oneself', and that 'all people develop their own belief system'.

As members of a 'dissenting' denomination, Unitarians were ostracized for their beliefs and persecuted, and it was not until 1813 (with the repeal of certain clauses of the Toleration Act) that Unitarianism finally became a legalized form of worship. Was Beatrix herself a Unitarian? This question will be addressed shortly.

Gaskell, for relaxation, often visited the Potters during their summer and autumn holidays at Dalguise on Scotland's River Tay for, like Mr Potter and Bertram, he was a keen fisherman. A delightful photograph exists, taken by Mr Potter, of Gaskell as an elderly gentleman with white hair and long, white sideburns, with his arm around the youthful Beatrix who (as usual) is to be seen wearing an 'Alice band' (as worn by Alice in *Through the Looking Glass*). Another shows Gaskell, sitting on a folding chair with his arm around the young Beatrix as she, attired in white dress and striped stockings, stands beside him. And yet another depicts the fishing party, relaxing in the garden at Dalguise after an excursion, with two enormous salmon at their feet, which are almost as long as the young Beatrix is tall.

Here it is interesting to note that Mr Potter's forbears also had associations with the Lake District. His kinsman Thomas Bayley Potter was a trader in textiles and owner of the largest mercantile business in Manchester. He was also a Unitarian, a Radical, a proponent of universal suffrage and a friend of Richard Cobden (economist and Radical and Liberal politician) and of John Bright. From 1865–95 he served as MP for Rochdale (in succession to Cobden). His wife was Mary, daughter of a cotton master, Samuel Ashton of Gee Cross, Hyde, Cheshire. From 1862 to 1874 he rented Pitnacree, a Scottish hunting lodge situated on the north bank of the River Tay, and also the 'shootings and lower fishings at [nearby] Dunfallandy'.[3]

Beatrix remembered, as a child, presenting Gaskell with a bunch of meadowsweet, to which he had replied, 'Thank you, dear,' and embraced her. She, in return for his kindness to her, subsequently knitted him a 'comforter', or blanket designed to keep the user warm.[4]

After Gaskell's death on 12 June 1884, Beatrix wrote sorrow-fully in her journal:

> There has always been a deep child-like affection between him and me. Shall I really never see him again? ... home is gone for me, the little girl [whom she once was] does not bound about now, and live in fairyland, and occasionally wonders ... what life means, and whether she shall ever feel sorrow. It is all gone, and he [Gaskell] is resting quietly with our fathers. I have begun the dark journey of life. Will it go on as darkly as it has begun?[5]

When autumn arrived, Beatrix's spirits still had not lifted and, on 12 October, she reminisced as follows:

> This day last year, how time moves and what it brings! So cold and stormy, and yet such gleams of peace and light making the darkness stranger and more dreary. How will it end for me?[6]

Notes

1. Reed, *Unitarian? What's that?* Para. 12.
2. Reed, *Unitarian? What's that?* Para. 38.
3. Matthew, H .C. G. and Brian Harrison, *Oxford Dictionary of National Biography*. Valuation Roll, 1870/71. Information kindly supplied by the A. K. Bell Library, Perth, Scotland.
4. Linder, *The Journal of Beatrix Potter from 1881–1897*, 12 June 1884, Note 32.
5. Linder, op. cit., 14 June 1884.
6. Ibid, 12 October 1884.

CHAPTER 7

A Deterioration in Health

B Y EARLY November 1884 it became clear that Beatrix's health was deteriorating: 'I am too tired to do anything. Began in my head, dreadfully tired and empty.'[1] On Christmas Day her sense of foreboding bordered on the morbid. 'I wonder how they all feel underground?' she asked, in an obvious reference to the dead.[2] At the end of March 1885 a clue as to the cause of Beatrix's chronic depression and lassitude appeared in her journal, when, referring to her hair, she stated:

> A lamentable falling off. Had my few remaining locks clipped short at Douglas's. Draughty. My hair nearly all came off since I was ill. Now that the sheep is shorn, I may say without pride that I have seldom seen a more beautiful head of hair than mine. Last summer it was very thick and within about four inches of my knees, being more than a yard long.[3]

Such loss of hair is one of the possible complications of glandular fever (infectious mononucleosis), first described by the German physician and paediatrician Emil Pfeiffer in 1889.[4] Early symptoms include a sore throat with swollen tonsils; high fever; excessive fatigue; loss of appetite and weight; enlarged and tender lymph glands; headache, and muscle pains. Generally, the symptoms disappear after a few weeks but post-viral fatigue syndrome may result, with chronic aches and pains in the limbs, poor concentration, depression, and lethargy. Symptoms may fluctuate and be exacerbated by exercise, excitement or stress.

Some weeks or months after the onset of the disease, a loss of hair may occur. Although the hair regrows it may never be as thick as it once was. (A portrait of Beatrix by Westmorland artist Delmar Banner, based on photographs of her in her mid-twenties, shows that, even by then, her hair had not regrown to its previous thickness.)

Presumably because of her illness, for which there was no cure but which usually ameliorates with time, Beatrix failed, between 20 April 1886 and the following December, to write a single word in her journal (and probably did no painting either). The anguish which this must have caused her cannot be over-estimated. Her journal provided her with a means of retreating into her secret world where she could express herself freely, set to rights the wrongs, real or imagined, of the world and create something that was entirely private – for her eyes, and for her eyes only. Writing the journal was a catharsis for her and an outlet for her creativity, and now this was denied her. However, as the months passed her health improved. Said she, of her holiday in 1886, spent as usual with her parents, this time in the Lake District:

> I never, all things considered, passed a pleasanter summer. We had not two wet days during the six weeks we stayed there.[5]

As if Beatrix had not suffered enough, she was overtaken, in April 1887, by another illness: one of such severity that it would affect her adversely for the rest of her life. She was now aged twenty, and the family were staying at the Lancashire seaside resort of Grange-over-Sands. The illness was rheumatic fever, another disease for which there was no cure.

A complication of rheumatic fever is damage to the mitral valve of the heart which may leak and/or become stenosed, with resultant cardiac failure or an irregularity of the heartbeat. Sure enough, in her letters, Beatrix frequently mentions how she has been obliged to rest, on account of the weakness of her heart, and a letter subsequently written by her several decades later shows that she was well aware of the cause of her disability. 'My heart has been too quick since I had rheumatic fever at 20', she declared.[6]

Notes

1. Linder, *The Journal of Beatrix Potter from 1881–1897*, 4 November 1884.
2. Ibid, 25 December 1884.
3. Ibid, 28 March 1885.
4. Glandular fever was first described by German physician and paediatrician Emil Pfeiffer in 1889. It is now known that the disease is caused by the Epstein Barr virus – named after Anthony Epstein and Yvonne Barr, together with Bert Achong, who discovered the virus in 1964. Even today, there is no cure.
5. Linder, *The Journal of Beatrix Potter from 1881–1897*, December 1886.
6. Beatrix to George Wilson (estate workman for the National Trust), 13 October 1943. Taylor, *Beatrix Potter's Letters*, p. 460.

CHAPTER 8

Sir John Millais

O NE DAY, when Beatrix was lying in bed ill with
'rheumatics' (i.e. rheumatic fever and its aftermath), she
received 'a little note'. It was from the famous painter Sir
John Everett Millais and his advice was that we must 'take the
world as we find it'.[1] Millais was a close friend of the Potter
family (Mr Potter being three years his junior). He not only
shared Mr Potter's love of Scotland and of fishing, he also took
Beatrix under his wing and became a mentor to her, in respect of
her own painting.

That autumn, when the Potters were taking their customary
holiday in Scotland, Millais and Quaker, orator and Radical
politician the Right Honourable John Bright MP joined them
at Dalguise where the menfolk 'enjoyed the sport' of salmon
fishing.[2] (Beatrix noted in her journal that Millais once caught a
salmon weighing forty-four pounds in the River Tay).[3] In that
year Millais painted his first portrait of British Liberal statesman
William Ewart (W. E.) Gladstone. In 1879 Millais and his family
stayed at Eastwood House, Dunkeld,[4] where Mr Potter visited
him and took photographs of him, his daughter, Effie and Lillie
Langtry. The latter photograph was mounted on card, signed by
the subjects and inscribed 'A Jersey pair', indicating that Millais
had not forgotten his Channel Island roots.

Unawed by Millais' reputation, Beatrix had no hesitation in giving a characteristically frank opinion of his work (not to him directly, of course, but in her journal, where she could express her thoughts freely). Of his painting of Mrs James Stern, which she viewed at the Royal Academy in June 1882, she opined that the subject is 'standing in front of too light a background ...'. And of his depiction of the young Miss Dorothy Thorpe she declared, 'A pretty picture, but like all Millais' other portraits this year, the face too pink, and the background too light.'[5] A decided opinion for one who was only fifteen years of age at the time! In that year Beatrix herself created, in pencil and sepia wash, the spiral staircase of St Mary's Tower, Birnam, which Millais and his family had rented some years previously.

In London, as in Scotland, the Millais and the Potter families frequently exchanged visits. On 6 March 1883 Beatrix noted that her father had, on her behalf, 'asked Mr Millais about mixing her paints, and he very kindly said what [paints] I should get'.[6] In May Mr Potter was anxious for his daughter to see two early paintings by Millais, *Isabella* and *Mariana*.[7] That November the seventeen-year-old Beatrix, accompanied by her parents, paid her first visit to the Millais' home at Palace Gate, Kensington (which was situated three-quarters of a mile to the north of Bolton Gardens).[8] This was something that she had often imagined doing, and it now seemed 'like a dream'. Mr Potter asked Millais for his opinion of 'Mrs Ward' [unidentified] as a potential art teacher for Beatrix. To which Millais, referring to Mrs Ward's teaching establishment, replied that 'it was the best place I [Beatrix] could go to'. Furthermore, if Mr Potter were to mention his name, then Beatrix would be 'attended to particularly'. And finally, said Beatrix, Millais told her that he 'hoped I would like it [i.e. her art lessons], and he'd come round one of these days and see what I was doing'.[9]

In mid-March 1884 Beatrix and her father again visited Millais and were shown his studio. He asked her how she was 'going on at Mrs A's' [another art teacher, also unidentified], to which Beatrix replied that, as yet, she had only had a dozen lessons.[10] In July, said Beatrix, 'Papa and Mamma went to a ball at the

Millais' a week or two since.' In the same month she said of her father:

> Papa has been photographing old Gladstone this morning at Mr Millais'. They kept off politics of course and talked about photography.[11]

Clearly, Millais, who was painting a portrait of W. E. Gladstone, had asked Mr Potter to provide a photograph of that gentleman. Gladstone, however, was not Mr Potter's favourite person, as will be seen! 'I never did so fine a portrait,' declared Millais a month later, having completed the work.[12] Beatrix, however, begged to differ, and declared in her journal (though not, of course, to Millais' face) that she was 'rather disappointed' with it.[13] On 16 July 1885, Gladstone 'set a seal on Millais' position as the country's most popular artist by having him created a baronet'.[14]

A famous painting by Millais, in which Mr Potter had a hand, was originally entitled, 'A Child's World', and subsequently 'Bubbles'. For this, the great painter had asked Mr Potter to take a photograph of his five-year-old grandson William Milbourne James, who would be the model for the child depicted in the painting.[15] (It was subsequently purchased by soap manufacturer A. and F. Pears and mass-produced as an advertisement poster for their product.)

The Millais had eight children, one of them being John Guille, 'Johnny', who was born in March 1865, and thus only sixteen months Beatrix's senior. In January 1886 Beatrix said scathingly of John, now aged twenty, 'This hopeful young person does very bad pen and inks of animals which he signs with his father's monogram.'[16] In fact, John became a notable wildlife artist and also a naturalist. On 7 March, Beatrix and her parents attended a private viewing of a Millais retrospective at the Grosvenor Gallery, where no less than 159 of his works were on show. And in her journal she gave a detailed critique, both of the exhibition itself, and of a number of the individual paintings. Said she, 'It seems to me unfortunate that the works are not chronologically arranged, they seem completely mixed up without rhyme or reason ...' However, it was her opinion that Millais' *Ophelia*, the tragic heroine of William Shakespeare's play *Hamlet*, was 'the most exquisite work in the collection, and probably one of the most marvellous pictures in the world'.[17]

In May 1890, when Beatrix's brother Bertram applied to the Athenaeum, Millais acted as his seconder. (He was finally elected to the club on 30 May 1906, after a six-year wait.)

London's Grosvenor Gallery, to which Beatrix and her parents were regular visitors, was situated in New Bond Street. Here, artists Walter Crane and Randolph Caldecott were regular exhibitors and both would play an important role when it came to Beatrix's own development as an artist. In June 1890 a group of Scottish artists held an exhibition at the Grosvenor Gallery, one of whom was Arthur Melville, one of the so-called 'Glasgow boys', who specialized in 'rural naturalism'. Beatrix, who disliked city life and became an avowed lover of the countryside, would have rejoiced in their paintings of rural families and landscapes, sheep, goats, geese and so forth. Given Beatrix and her father's love of all things Scottish, they would undoubtedly have attended this exhibition. (From Beatrix's journal, it is known that the Potter family was in London at the time of this exhibition.) One painting, in particular, may have caught her eye. It was entitled 'Cabbage Garden' by Arthur Melville and in it a gardener is depicted leaning on his spade, surrounded by a veritable sea of magnificent cabbages while he engages a young lady in conversation. The possible significance of this painting will be discussed shortly.

On 13 August 1896 Millais died at the age of sixty-seven. This was sixteen days after Beatrix's thirtieth birthday, and only six months after the great painter had been elected President of the Royal Academy. He was buried in St Paul's Cathedral. (His wife, Effie, died at the end of the following year.) Nine months earlier the great painter had described Beatrix as his 'little friend'. Of the late Millais, she said:

> He gave me the kindest encouragement with my drawings
> ... but he really paid me a compliment for he said that

41

'plenty of people can *draw*, but you and my son Johnny have observation'.

In her opinion he was 'an honest fine man', and she would 'always have a most affectionate remembrance' of him. And this, despite the fact that Millais had once told her that although she was:

> a little like his daughter Carrie [Alice Sophie Caroline, born four years prior to Beatrix in 1862], at that time a fine handsome girl ... my face was spoiled by the length of my nose and upper lip.[18]

However, in one comment which Beatrix made after Millais' death, there was sadness, tinged with a hint of envy. This referred to the Millais family. Said she, 'In London society they were [seen] in a different light, we in none at all ...'[19]

Notes

1. Linder, *The Journal of Beatrix Potter from 1881–1897*, 13 August 1896.
2. Ibid, p. 277.
3. Linder, op. cit., 27 October 1884.
4. Millais, op. cit., p. 277.
5. Linder, op. cit., 10 June 1882.
6. Ibid, 6 March 1883.
7. Ibid, 2 May 1883.
8. Ibid, 11 November 1883.
9. Ibid, 11 November 1883.
10. Ibid, 14 March 1884.
11. Ibid, 8 July 1884, 28 July 1884.
12. Millais, op. cit., Millais to his wife. 1 August 1884.
13. Linder, op. cit., 9 May 1885.
14. H. C. G. Matthew and Brian Harrison, *Oxford Dictionary of National Biography*.
15. Linder, op. cit., 15 November 1885.
16. Ibid, 29 January 1886.
17. Ibid, 7 March 1886.
18. Ibid, 13 August 1896.
19. Ibid, 13 August 1896.

CHAPTER 9

Dr James Martineau:
Beatrix and Religion

ANOTHER of Mr Potter's former tutors at Manchester New College was Professor of Mental and Moral Philosophy and Political Economy, was James Martineau, the author of several books on religion who argued in his booklet *The Rationale of Religion* (published in 1836) that religious truth must not run contrary to reason. Like Gaskell, Martineau became Mr Potter's lifelong friend.

Martineau welcomed developments in the field of science which took place in the nineteenth century, declaring that 'The architects of science have raised over us a nobler temple, and the hierophants of Nature [have] introduced us to a sublimer worship'.[1] In regard to the 'miracles and supernatural events' described in the Bible, he declared that Christianity could not rest on a literalistic reading of the New Testament's stories, to which, in the evaluation of that religion, little or no weight should be attached:

> Rather it depends on a deeper, living appreciation of the 'mind of Christ' – feeling and following what he felt and followed, standing 'with him at the same spring'.[2]

This was not to say that God's position was in any way diminished, for Martineau also declared that 'The world and its fullness are thine [i.e. God's]: our portion thereof may we hold, not in wanton self-will, but reverently, as of thee.'[3]

When, in 1853, Manchester New College relocated to London, Martineau continued to lecture at that institution, even though this meant commuting from Manchester until finally, in 1857, he too relocated to the capital. That was the same year in which Mr Potter moved to London (having been called to the Bar), where he was able to maintain contact with his *Alma Mater* by attending and participating in college debates.

From 1859 Martineau combined his duties as college lecturer with that of co-minister and, later, minister at Little Portland Street [Unitarian] Chapel, Westminster. Here, the Potters came regularly to worship, the chapel being four and a half miles from their home at Bolton Gardens. Mr Potter is described as 'a generous subscriber to its funds and to those of the Portland [Chapel] Schools.'[4] When, a decade later in 1869, Manchester New College's Principal, the Reverend Dr John James Tayler died, Martineau succeeded him, and retained the post until his retirement in 1885. He himself died in 1900.

Beatrix referred several times, in her journal, to visits made by herself and her family to the home of the Reverend Martineau and his wife, Helen, at Gordon Square, Bloomsbury:[5]

> I think Papa has a greater respect and admiration for Dr. Martineau as to his intellect and character than any other man. I have heard him say he is the only man to whom he would trust his conscience implicitly in religious matters, as having a certain reliance on his clearness and good sense.[6]

Mr Potter's high opinion of Martineau was shared by Beatrix's uncle, Sir Henry Roscoe, who declared that 'a more noble-minded man never breathed ...'. Roscoe also described the 'admirable manner in which Martineau used to read Scott's novels and poetry to ... family and friends', a quality which would have endeared him to Beatrix.[7]

44

By April 1892 the Potters had transferred their allegiance to Essex Church, Kensington, which was more conveniently situated, being less than a mile to the north of their home at Bolton Gardens. (Essex Church had started life as Essex Chapel, Essex Street, Strand, where, as previously mentioned, Britain's first Unitarian congregation had been established in 1774. In 1874 Essex Chapel relocated to Kensington, and on 4 May 1887, new premises were opened and renamed Essex Church.) Of Essex Church, Beatrix was not enamoured, for having attended service there in February 1896, she declared:

> I cannot say I feel the slightest interest or pleasure in that Chapel [she insisted on its former appellation], apart from going [there] with my father.[8]

It is interesting to speculate that whilst sitting, albeit reluctantly, in a pew at Essex Church, Beatrix may have caught sight of Charles Darwin (naturalist and co-originator of the Theory of Evolution, who frequently worshipped there) and of Sir Charles Lyell (Scottish geologist, who was a regular member of its congregation).[9]

If anyone believed that Beatrix would embrace Unitarianism simply because her forbears had embraced it, or because Gaskell and Martineau, two of her favourite elderly gentlemen acquaintances, were two of its leading lights, then they were mistaken, for (in her journal, where she could be certain that her thoughts would always remain private) she summed up her attitude to religion thus:

> All outward forms of religion are almost useless, and are the cause of endless strife.[10] What do Creeds matter, what possible difference does it make to anyone today whether the doctrine of the resurrection is correct or incorrect, or the miracles ...[11]

As for Unitarianism in particular, she declared:

> I shall always call myself a Unitarian because of my father and grandmother, but for the Unitarians as a Dissenting

body, as I have known them in London, I have no respect. Their creed is apt to be a timid, illogical compromise, and their forms of Service, a badly performed imitation of the Church. Their total want of independence and backbone is shown by the way they call their chapels 'churches', and drag in the word Christian. We are not Christians in the commonly accepted sense of the term.[12]

Nevertheless, she had her own, simple, homespun faith, her advice being 'Believe there is a great power silently working all things for good, behave yourself and never mind the rest.'[13]

Of other dissenting religions, Beatrix stated that she 'always had a strong prejudice in favour of the Quakers'.[14] However, 'I think it was Dr [Samuel] Johnson, at all events I like to think it was, who said that wise men are of the same religion. I always think of Dr Johnson as a Quaker,' said she, referring to the famous writer, critic, lexicographer and conversationalist.[15]

Some aspects of religious worship Beatrix *did* enjoy. For example, in August 1895, having attended a Congregationalist service at Troutbeck Chapel in the Lake District, presided over by the Reverend Parker, she said that she found the Congregationalists 'more liberal than the Methodists and the Baptists' and considered the singing of two of her favourite hymns to be 'very sweet.'[16]

As for the Anglican faith, there were aspects of it that brought her to a state of abject rage and indignation. For example, in September 1884, whilst holidaying at Bush Hall, Hertfordshire (the property of Lord Salisbury), she was appalled to learn that at Hatfield, in that county, it was a 'common superstition' that if a child had not been baptized into the Christian faith, then not only would it not be given a Christian burial, but it would also go to hell.

How can anyone believe that the power above us – call it Jehovah, Allah, Trinity, what they will – is a just and merciful father [who] will yet create a child, a little rosebud, the short-lived pain of its mother's heart, only to assign it after a few days of innocence to eternal torment.[17]

The way in which Beatrix was able to evaluate, dispassionately, the Potters' and the Leechs' great family tradition of Unitarianism is a reflection of the power of her critical faculties and strength of mind. Nonetheless, in 1912, and despite her reservations about Unitarianism, she visited Stalybridge where she opened its Unitarian Church's annual, four-day bazaar, a function which her father had fulfilled twelve years earlier.[18]

Mr Potter's Unitarian faith, however (and presumably Mrs Potter's also), remained undimmed. He is described as 'a devoted member' of Essex Church, and also:

> a contributor to the funds of Glossop Chapel [Dinting, Derbyshire], built with the financial support of his father, and a constant supporter of the Stalybridge Chapel and Schools.[19]

Notes

1. Martineau, 1890, *The Seat of Authority in Religion*.
2. Reed, *Beatrix Potter's Unitarian Context*, p. 5.
3. Martineau, *Common Prayer for Christian Worship*.
4. *The Inquirer*, Memorial Notice, 16 May 1914.
5. Linder, *The Journal of Beatrix Potter from 1881–1897*, p. 114.
6. Linder, op. cit., 19 November 1884.
7. Roscoe, *The Life & Experiences of Sir Henry Enfield Roscoe*, p. 21.
8. Linder, op. cit., 23 February 1896.
9. Perris, 1900. *Sketch of the History of Little Portland Street Chapel*.
10. Linder, op. cit., 30 September 1884, p. 104.
11. Ibid, 30 September 1884.
12. Ibid, 23 February 1896.
13. Ibid, 30 September 1884.
14. Ibid, 1892.
15. Ibid, April 1892.
16. Ibid, 18 August 1895.
17. Ibid, 30 September 1884.
18. *The Inquirer*, 30 July 1966.
19. *The Inquirer*, Memorial Notice, 16 May 1914.

CHAPTER 10

Beatrix in Her Twenties

A S BEATRIX'S health improved, so also did her spirits, and by the early 1890s her former zest, enthusiasm, creativity, and natural inquisitiveness had also returned. Pets continued to play a large part in her life, and having little or no contact with her peers she depended upon the former for company and friendship. She even took them on holiday with her, transporting each particular species in its own little cage. For example, she described how, in late July 1892, she transported her rabbit, Benjamin, by train 'in a covered basket in the washplace [of the train]' from her home in London to Heath Park, Birnam, Perthshire. Benjamin, however, 'proved scared and bit the family'.[1] Having arrived at her destination she stated, regarding Benjamin, 'I walk him about with a leather strap [leash].' This was much to the amusement of the local people.[2]

Beatrix's descriptions of rabbits in general, and of Benjamin in particular, reveal not only that she was a keen observer of her rabbit's antics, but also that she had an equally keen insight into his character. Benjamin was, she said:

> at one moment amiably sentimental to the verge of silliness, at the next, the upsetting of a jug or tea-cup which he immediately takes upon himself, will convert him into a

48

demon, throwing himself on his back, scratching and spluttering. If I can lay hold of him without being bitten, within half a minute he is licking my hands as though nothing has happened.

He is an abject coward, but believes in bluster, could stare our old dog out of countenance, chase a cat that has turned tail.

'I do not on the average care for dogs,'[4] wrote Beatrix, but she always kept a dog of one kind or another, spaniels, terriers, and latterly sheepdogs and Pekineses being some of her favourite breeds. And in numerous photographs she was to be seen in the company of dogs and, as often as not, cuddling them.

Of her faithful pony, 'Mistress Nelly', who pulled the gig which took her on her various excursions and expeditions, Beatrix could not speak too highly:

There may not be much style, but commend me to a horse which will stand still, go any distance, face the steepest road and never stumble once the whole season, and take an amusing and intelligent interest in geography.[5]

In Scotland Beatrix loved to engage country people in conversation and listen to them as they reminisced. Such a person was Kitty MacDonald of Inver, who was the Potters' laundress when they stayed at Dalguise. Beatrix described Kitty as:

a comical, round little old woman ... Her memory goes back for seventy years and I really believe she is prepared to enumerate the articles of her first [laundry] wash in [18]'71 [The year of the Potters' first visit to Dalguise.][6] The joy of converse with old Katie [Kitty] was to draw her out to talk of the days when she was a wee bit [little] lassie – herding the kine [cows] ... the old woman wouldn't dwell upon hard weather and storms; she spoke of sunshine and clouds ... A bonny life it was, but it can never come back.[7]

However, it was the menfolk whom she found most interesting. David Wood, for example, the local shoemaker, was also an entymologist who presented her 'out of his hat ... [with] about two dozen buff-tip caterpillars, collected on the road'[8] and James Malloch, a retired master mason 'used to waylay us children in the woods and go for long walks, telling us stories of caves and whisky stills'. (This was a reference to the days when the local people used to distil whisky illicitly.)[9]

In London in February the following year, 1893, the twenty-seven-year-old Beatrix visited the home of her near neighbours, the elderly John and Elizabeth Paget of 28 The Boltons (he being a retired barrister and Metropolitan Police magistrate) and their two daughters. This was to return some of Elizabeth Ann, known as 'Nina', Paget's 'infinite number of guinea-pigs', which she had borrowed in order to draw them. From Beatrix's account it might be assumed that Nina was a child. In fact, she was then aged fifty-two![10]

In June 1894 Beatrix visited Harescombe Grange near Stroud in Gloucestershire – the home of her cousin, Caroline Hutton (who was descended from her father's 'Crompton' forbears), having for once, been let off the parental leash.

> I used to go to my grandmother's, and once I went for a week to Manchester but I have not been away independently for five years. It was an event.

In respect of Caroline, whom she had evidently not met before, Beatrix said, 'I don't think I ever became so completely fond of anyone in so short a time.' Many years later, Beatrix would describe, to Caroline, those qualities which she most admired and which were characteristic of her paternal ancestors: 'Crompton tenacity, obstinate, indomitable to the end.'[11] However, the two of them differed in that, whilst Beatrix was of the opinion that 'a happy marriage is the crown of a woman's life', Caroline appeared to value her independence. And Beatrix was equally bemused when this 'nice-looking lady' proclaimed 'a pronounced dislike of babies and all child cousins'.[12] Caroline wrote of Beatrix's visit:

> I am always glad, that in spite of her [Beatrix's] mother's objections I managed to get her to my old home. She [Mrs Potter] said, 'B. [Beatrix] was so apt to be sick and to faint; and I, regardless of the truth, said I was quite accustomed to all that ...[13]

For Beatrix, it was books and, in particular, those of her favourite novelist, Sir Walter Scott, which helped to fill the void caused by the paucity of childhood playmates. For example, in September 1894, when she and her family were on holiday at Lennel, near Coldstream in the Scottish Borders (the southern region of Scotland adjacent to the border with England), she described a visit to Smailholm Tower near Kelso, a fifteenth century 'peel tower' (one designed to protect its occupants from sporadic raids by the English) which belonged to the Scott family, and of which he, Sir Walter, 'sang so sweetly'. She also mentioned the River Tweed 'winding about the last resting place of Sir Walter Scott' [which was Dryburgh Abbey, where he was buried in the family tomb beside his wife, Charlotte].[14] And her journal revealed that Scott's novels were very much in her mind as she followed in his footsteps and explored the Border country. This love affair with his writings would be a lifelong one, for in later years she was to declare that 'I have gone back to Scott's novels with never failing pleasure.'[15]

On 6 October 1894 she told how she had found some interesting fossils, having learnt how to select potential fossil-bearing stones and split them with a cold chisel. She discovered a particularly interesting one, which she identified as *arancarioxylon*. And she enjoyed creating illustrations, in watercolour, of the specimens of fungi which she had found. At Lennel, however, Beatrix and her mother were again at loggerheads, this time because Mrs Potter had vetoed a proposed visit by Beatrix's younger cousins, Caroline and Mary Hutton from Stroud in

Gloucestershire, on the grounds that the accommodation was not in a fit state.

> There is only one spare bedroom, and that's so dirty that no one will sleep therein, but the sting of my annoyance was that this was regarded as a convenient excuse. [Beatrix was also annoyed] ... because my mother will not order the carriage in the morning or make up her mind, and if I say I should like to go out after lunch I'm keeping her in and if she does not go and I have missed the chance of a long drive, it is provoking.[16]

Nonetheless, two days later Beatrix obtained the use of the carriage and 'had a delightful drive, defying the enemy [her mother] and after all got home in time for lunch'.[17] There were, however, other occasions when Beatrix and her mother ventured out together, as when, during the same holiday, they visited Twizell, where Beatrix imagined 'heavily armed men' crossing the muddy ford on the way to the Battle of Flodden (a battle between the Scots and the English in 1513).[18] And, said Beatrix, when the Potters paid a visit to Berwick, situated at the mouth of the River Tweed, 'Mamma and I went down to the beach ... where there were washerwomen spreading out clothes and people sitting on the grass in the hot glow [of the sun]'.[19]

Sadly, that particular holiday did not end well for, on 10 October 1894, Beatrix observed that her mother was not in a good humour, and had expressed 'a most hearty aversion and prejudice to the whole affair [i.e. to their holiday]'. Said Beatrix, 'It is somewhat trying to pass a season of enjoyment in the company of persons who are constantly on the outlook for matters of complaint.' In fact, she [Beatrix] and Elizabeth, the housemaid, were 'the only persons who were currently pleased ...' with the visit.[20]

Mrs Potter did not always enjoy good health and during her frequent bouts of illness the task of looking after her fell to Beatrix, who always did her duty, even if she did not particularly enjoy it. In October 1895, for example, when 'Mamma' began to haemorrhage and remained upstairs in her room for almost a fortnight, Beatrix commented, ruefully:

> I had a weary time ... There is supposed to be some angelic sentiment in tending the sick, but personally, I should not associate angels with castor oil and emptying slops.[21]

At Sawrey in the Lake District in July 1896 Beatrix was in excellent spirits when she recorded in her journal, 'I am thirty this day ... I feel much younger at thirty than I did at twenty; firmer and stronger both in mind and body.'[22] In other words, her glandular fever was a thing of the past. However, the same could not be said of her rheumatic fever, which left its legacy. In that year, some of her drawings appeared in *Nister's Holiday Annual for 1896*.

What efforts did Mr and Mrs Potter make to help Beatrix find a husband? For a young woman to enter fashionable society it was first necessary for her to be presented to Her Majesty Queen Victoria at a ceremony conducted four times each year at the Court Drawing Rooms of Buckingham Palace. (Beatrix, in her journal, actually mentioned that, on 18 March 1885, when she and her mother were travelling along Buckingham Palace Road, 'Her Majesty was having a Drawing-room' at that very time.)[23] Those eligible to be presented at Court included the daughters of the aristocracy (who had the privilege of being kissed by HM The Queen), of the gentry, of clergy, of naval and military officers, of professional men, such as physicians and surgeons (but not general practitioners), of barristers (but not solicitors), of merchants, of bankers, of members of the Stock Exchange, and of those involved in large-scale commercial operations. As Beatrix was the daughter of a barrister there would, therefore, have been no impediment to her being presented at Court. It would then have been open to her to participate in the London season, which commenced in May, with the annual exhibition of paintings at the Royal Academy of Art. As an artist, this would have suited Beatrix admirably. This was followed by a plethora of court balls and concerts, private balls, dances and parties, and sporting events, such as horse racing at Ascot races and the Henley Regatta.

The fact was, however, that Beatrix had very little self-confidence in this regard and may have resisted such a course of action. This was revealed by her in her journal, when she compared herself to her cousin, Kate, daughter of Mr Potter's eldest brother, Edmund and his wife, Mary. If her [Beatrix's] father, she said, had possessed:

> a beautiful daughter like Kate there is no doubt he could marry her very well, he is intimate with all the rich and respectable Unitarians' families, or if ambitious, he could easily take her into fashionable society.[24]

This implies that Beatrix did not consider herself as possessing sufficient beauty to enter into high society. (Lillie Langtry, an acquaintance of the Potters, was a classic example of how someone could capitalize on their beauty by doing just that; though in her case, the outcome was not an altogether happy one.) However, it should also be said that there is no evidence that Mrs and Mrs Potter, for their part, made any attempt to introduce Beatrix to a possible suitor.

Notes

1. Linder, *The Journal of Beatrix Potter from 1881–1897*, 26 July 1892.
2. Ibid, 4 August 1892.
3. Ibid, 30 October 1892.
4. Ibid, 1892.
5. Ibid, 1 October 1894.
6. Ibid, 1 August 1892.
7. Linder, *A History of the Writings of Beatrix Potter*, p. 159.
8. Linder, *The Journal of Beatrix Potter from 1881–1897*, 1 September 1892.
9. Ibid, 13 October 1892.
10. Ibid, 5 February 1893.
11. Beatrix to Caroline Clark, 15 February 1937. Taylor, *Beatrix Potter's Letters*, p. 384.
12. Linder, *The Journal of Beatrix Potter from 1881–1897*, June 1894.
13. Mrs Clark (née Hutton) of Ulva. Letter to Margaret Lane, quoted in Lane, *The Magic Years of Beatrix Potter*, p. 79.

14. Linder, *The Journal of Beatrix Potter from 1881–1897*, 17 September 1894.
15. Beatrix to Andrew McKay, 24 February 1930. In Morse, *Beatrix Potter's Americans: Selected Letters*, p. 34.
16. Linder, *The Journal of Beatrix Potter from 1881–1897*, 11 September 1894.
17. Ibid, 13 September 1894.
18. Ibid, p. 335.
19. Ibid, p. 337.
20. Ibid, 10 October 1894.
21. Ibid, 11 October 1895.
22. Ibid, 28 July 1896.
23. Ibid, 18 March 1885.
24. Ibid, 7 September 1885.

CHAPTER 11

Charles McIntosh

O NE DAY in 1871, when she and her parents were on
summer holiday at Dalguise House, Perthshire, Scotland,
Beatrix, who was then a child approaching her fifth
birthday, encountered a person who would later greatly influence
her life.[1]

Beatrix waited patiently beneath a copper beech tree for the
postman to arrive; her parents having sent her to 'get the letters'.
And, suddenly, there he was, in her words 'swinging up the
avenue with long strides and head down ... Perhaps I remember
this because, on that first occasion, I ran away – I don't know
which of us was the shyest'. It was not surprising that Beatrix
was somewhat overawed by the postman who stood 'six feet two
and a half inches in his stockinged soles', walked with a 'quick
step' and a 'slight stoop', and blew a whistle to indicate his
approach.[2] His name was Charles McIntosh and, as well as being
a postman, he was a man of many talents.

The son of a handloom weaver, fiddle player, and music
teacher, McIntosh was born at Inver, near Birnam, Perthshire on
27 March 1839, two years after Queen Victoria had acceded to
the throne. He was educated at the Free Church School, Birnam,
and at the Royal Grammar School, Dunkeld. He worshipped at
Little Dunkeld (Presbyterian) Church where, following in the

56

footsteps of his father and grandfather, he became precentor. Like Beatrix, he was a polymath: a composer and arranger of music, an amateur ornithologist, geologist, meteorologist, and, finally, an acknowledged expert on fungi, mosses, and other aspects of natural science, for which he became known as 'The Perthshire Naturalist'.

Beatrix may not have noticed that McIntosh had no fingers or thumb on his left hand, as he was expert at concealing the fact. This was the result of an accident, which he had sustained fourteen years previously whilst working at a saw mill; hence his enforced change of occupation. Almost seven years later, in March 1887 (by which time Beatrix was aged twenty), Mr Potter, who knew of McIntosh's interest in fungi, wrote to him as follows:

> Mr Rupert Potter has during the last year purchased and received from Rev. J. Stevenson of Glamis the 2 volumes of his work on 'British Fungi', published by Messrs Blackwood of Edinburgh & the book is apparently very valuable and interesting to anyone who knows enough to understand it.[3] Mr Potter remembers that Mr C. McIntosh is a scientific authority in that department of knowledge & he therefore writes to ask Mr McIntosh whether he would accept the work from Mr Potter if Mr McIntosh has not already got it.[4]

Having received a reply in the affirmative, Mr Potter wrote once again to McIntosh, to say that he had arranged for his bookseller to forward the volumes to him:

> which his friend Sir E. [Edward] Fry [British judge and author of *British Mosses*, published in 1892] & the Secretary of the Linnean Society[5] have recommended to Mr Potter as the most recent and suitable books on that subject which he can give himself the pleasure of sending. Mr Potter & his daughter all hope to know that Mr McIntosh will find the books interesting.[6]

What had prompted Mr Potter to perform this generous gesture? Perhaps he was anxious to assist a person who, with courage and determination, had overcome great difficulties and whose talent he recognized. For example, despite the injury to his hand, McIntosh had taught himself to play the violoncello, instead of the violin as had previously been the case. This he did by sliding his 'truncated hand ... up and down the strings'.[7] ('The Braes of Tullymet' – a 'brae' being a bank or slope – was a traditional Scottish strathspey which McIntosh's father and namesake, Charles, played on the fiddle, as, no doubt, did his son, on the violoncello.)[8] Another reason may have been that Mr Potter hoped that McIntosh would be of help to his daughter, Beatrix, who was also passionately interested in the study of fungi, for the postman was a born teacher who organized open-air lessons in botany for children on Sundays, and who assisted in the excursions made by both the senior and junior sections of the Perthshire Society of Natural Science.

From an early age Beatrix loved flowers, not only as objects of beauty, but as subjects for scientific research. In addition to collecting, photographing and examining under the microscope specimens from the natural world, Beatrix would also draw and paint them, make meticulous notes, and even develop her own theories about them. On 12 October 1884, when she was aged eighteen, she received from her 'loving Grandmother', Jessie Potter (née Crompton) a present, the 1882 edition of *British Wild Flowers* by C. Pierpoint Johnson with illustrations by John E. Sowerby.

For Beatrix, however, it was fungi which provided the greatest fascination. In the summer of 1887 she was with her family at Lingholm, Derwentwater in the English Lake District, where she painted two specimens of fungi (which presumably she had discovered locally), namely *Stropharia aeruginosa* and *Clitocybe geotropa*.

In 1892, more than two decades after she had first set eyes on McIntosh, Beatrix, now aged twenty-six, expressed a desire to meet with him again. This was in order to discuss with him her drawings of various rare species of fungi which she had discovered. Two years previously, in 1890, McIntosh had retired from postal work (at the age of fifty-one), having suffered repeated attacks of pleurisy, brought on by his 'exposure to all kinds of weather'.[9] He had served as a postman for thirty-two years, during which time he had delivered the mail on foot, every day except Sundays, his route taking him from Dunkeld, along the west bank of the River Tay to Kinnaird House and back, a journey that totalled sixteen miles.

Beatrix's wish was granted on 29 October 1892 when she and her parents were staying at Heath Park, Birnam, not far from McIntosh's home at Inver. She described McIntosh, variously, as a 'mysterious person', 'uncouth', a 'scared, startled scarecrow', and like 'a damaged lamp post'. However, she revealed the tender side of her nature by saying, 'I would not make fun of him for worlds.' Moreover, her subsequent correspondence with him revealed her great respect for him, and with Beatrix respect was something which was not easily earned.

> When we discussed funguses he became quite excited and spoke with quite poetical feelings about their exquisite colours. [I found him] conscientiously accurate [in his statements on the subject] as befitted a correspondent of the scholarly Mr Barclay of Glamis.[10]

Here Beatrix made what author and mycologist Dr Mary Noble described as 'a curious mistake' in that, instead of Barclay, what she had meant to write was 'Dr Stevenson of Glamis' (a copy of whose newly published and highly authoritative work in two volumes, entitled *British Fungi [Hymenomycetes]*, her father had previously presented to McIntosh. By November 1893 Beatrix herself had acquired a copy of this book).[11]

The Reverend Dr John Stevenson was born at Coupar Angus (situated ten miles south-west of Glamis) in Perthshire in 1836. In 1859 he was licensed as a preacher in the established Church of Scotland and, in 1873, was appointed Minister to the Parish of Glamis.

Mr Stevenson began his residence at Glamis when interest in fungi was very strong; and fortunately near the Manse [house of the minister] was ground peculiarly rich for several years in numerous forms of the larger fungi. Soon he was prominent amongst the most successful discoverers of additions to the British lists of fungi ... [He also] made a careful personal study especially of the Hymenomycetes, and was recognized as an authority on these fungi. He took an active part in the foundation of the British Cryptogamic Society in 1874 [of which he served as honorary secretary] ...[12]

Finally, McIntosh's biographer, Henry Coates, provides confirmation that the former was indeed a 'correspondent' of Stevenson, when he states that:

Sometimes, though not often, a more than usually puzzling specimen [of fungus] would be sent to the Revd John Stevenson at Glamis [by McIntosh] for elucidation, but only after all sources of information at hand had been exhausted.[13]

Subsequent to her meeting with McIntosh on 29 October 1892, Beatrix, at the latter's request, made some drawings of fungi for him which she sent to him from London by post. And as a quid pro quo he sent specimens of fungi down from Scotland to London by parcel post. Said she, writing in the third person about her drawings, 'Miss Potter ... hopes Mr McIntosh will think them sufficiently accurate to be worth his acceptance.'[14] In another letter to McIntosh, Beatrix described how, at the Natural History Museum, she had seen 'a number of portfolios with drawings & printed plates' of fungi, but she bewailed the fact that there was no one present there to give any information about them.[15]

According to Dr Mary Noble, when, in the autumn of 1893, a rare fungus was discovered in the grounds of Eastwood House on the River Tay at Dunkeld:

There is every reason to believe that C. M. [McIntosh] was sent for. He tentatively identified it as *Strobilomyces* but also sent a specimen to Revd John Stevenson at Glamis who replied confirming its identity and adding 'a very good find'.[16]

Thereafter, however, it appears that although Beatrix and McIntosh continued to communicate with one another, they did not again meet in person. Meanwhile, Beatrix's pursuit of rare and beautiful fungi continued unabated. In August 1894, while staying at Lennel, Beatrix described visiting a wood near Hatchednize where:

the fungus [fungi] starred the ground apparently in thousands, a dozen sorts in sight at once ... I found upwards of twenty sorts in a few minutes, *Cortinarius* and the handsome *Lactarius deliciosus* being conspicuous, and joy of joys, the spiky *Gomphidius glutinosus*, a round, slimy, purple head among the moss, which I took up carefully with my old cheese-knife, and turning [it] over saw the slimy veil. There is extreme complacency [by which she presumably means satisfaction] in finding a totally new species for the first time.[17]

The following month she and her father visited Smailholm Tower near Kelso and, whilst Mr Potter indulged himself in his hobby of photography, Beatrix went hunting for fungi. She found 'much white *Hygrophorus* and some gigantic red ones, also a *Cortinarius*, brittle and graceful on bleached horse-dung in the bog'.[18] In early October she described making 'about forty careful drawings of funguses ...'.[19]

By 1896 Beatrix was employing a microscope, set at 'X600 magnification', to assist with her detailed drawings and water-colour paintings of fungi. (She had acquired the instrument from her brother, Bertram, when he went away to boarding school, but would later obtain a new one for herself.)

When, in November 1896, Beatrix returned home to London from Sawrey in the Lake District, she 'was so engrossed by the difficulty of transporting my precious fungi that I paid no particular attention to the journey'.[20] At about this time Mr Potter purchased for Beatrix 'that very expensive book', a work entitled *Botanische Untersuchungen über Schimmelpilze (Botanical Investigations into Moulds)* by German botanist and mycologist (Julius) Oskar Brefeld.[21] However, she found Brefeld's style of writing to be 'discursive and unstable ...'.[22]

In February 1897 Beatrix proudly told McIntosh, 'I have grown between 40 & 55 sorts of [fungal] spore.'[23] He, for his part, suggested to her that she might improve her illustrations and make them 'more perfect as botanical drawings' by sketching the various parts of her fungi individually.[24]

It is doubtful whether Beatrix ever visited McIntosh at his home at Inver. However, a description of it is given by John Ramsbottom, Keeper of Botany at the British Museum (Natural History), who, in 1921, was invited by William Barclay and by John Robert Matthews, to visit 'Charlie' at the 'lowly Inver cottage in which he was born ...'. (Barclay, who is described as 'an old friend' of McIntosh, was a local headmaster from Perth who, from 1907, served for eleven years as President of the Perthshire Natural History Society, whereas Matthews was Lecturer in Botany at Edinburgh University.) Here, they discovered:

> A living room in which the principal items were a harmonium with some manuscript [i.e. musical scores], a violoncello in the corner, a table near the window with a microscope, a few books, and an agaric ... A striking impression [was obtained] of the towering, gaunt, kindly Scot.[25]

McIntosh, who had lived alone in his cottage since the death of his mother in 1896, died on 5 January 1922 at the age of eighty-two. During his lifetime he had discovered no fewer than seventeen varieties of 'new fungi'.[26]

Notes

1. Although Beatrix stated that it was in 1870 that she had first encountered McIntosh, it appears that in this she was mistaken and that she had, in fact, first encountered him in the following year, 1871, when she was staying at Dalguise. This may be deduced from the fact that whereas Dalguise was on the postman's regular route Tullymet was not. If this was indeed an error on Beatrix's part then she may be forgiven, for no less than fifty-three years had elapsed since the event and her recollection of it. Coates, *A Perthshire Naturalist*, p. 123.

2. Coates, pp. 124–6.

3. Beatrix to Charles McIntosh. 19 November 1893. Coppins, B. J. (editor). 1987. Notes from the Royal Botanic Garden, Edinburgh, 44(3). Article by Noble: *Beatrix Potter, Naturalist & Mycologist and Charles McIntosh, the 'Perthshire Naturalist'*, p. 612.

4. Rupert Potter to Charles McIntosh. 3 March 1887. Coppins, B. J. (editor). 1987. Notes from the Royal Botanic Garden, Edinburgh, 44(3). Article by Noble: *Beatrix Potter, Naturalist & Mycologist and Charles McIntosh, the 'Perthshire Naturalist'*, p. 609.

5. In fact, there were two secretaries of the Linnean Society in the year 1892: Benjamin Daydon Jackson and W. Percy Sladen. Information kindly supplied by the Linnean Society of London.

6. Rupert Potter to Charles McIntosh. Undated. Coppins, B. J. (editor). 1987. *Notes from the Royal Botanic Garden, Edinburgh*. 44(3). Article by Noble: *Beatrix Potter, Naturalist & Mycologist and Charles McIntosh, the 'Perthshire Naturalist'*, p. 610.

7. Coates, op. cit., p. 68.

8. Ibid, p. 123.

9. Ibid, p. 82.

10. Linder, *The Journal of Beatrix Potter from 1881–1897*, 29 October 1892.

11. Noble, 1984. *Beatrix Potter and her Funguses*. Beatrix Potter Studies I, pp. 41–6.

12. Harvie-Brown, J. A. James, W. H. Trail and William Eagle Clarke (editors). 1904. *The Annals of Scottish Natural History*. No. 49. Revd John Stevenson, LL.D. Obituary.

13. Coates, op. cit., pp. 173–4.

14. Beatrix to Charles McIntosh, 10 December 1892. Coppins, B. J. (editor). 1987. Notes from the Royal Botanic Garden, Edinburgh, 44(3). Article by Noble: *Beatrix Potter, Naturalist & Mycologist and Charles McIntosh, the 'Perthshire Naturalist'*. p. 610.

15. Beatrix to Charles McIntosh, letter believed to have been written in 1893. Coppins, B. J. (editor). 1987. Notes from the Royal Botanic Garden, Edinburgh, 44(3). Article by Noble: *Beatrix Potter, Naturalist & Mycologist and Charles McIntosh, the 'Perthshire Naturalist'*. p. 612.

16. Coppins, B. J. (editor). 1987. *Notes from the Royal Botanic Garden, Edinburgh*. 44(3). Article by Noble: *Beatrix Potter, Naturalist & Mycologist and Charles McIntosh, the 'Perthshire Naturalist'*, Note 52.
17. Linder, op. cit., 18 August 1894.
18. Ibid, 25 September 1894.
19. Ibid, 10 October 1894.
20. Ibid, 17 November 1896.
21. Ibid, 3 December 1896.
22. Ibid, 26 December 1896.
23. Beatrix to Charles McIntosh. 22 February 1897. Coppins, B. J. (editor). 1987. Notes from the Royal Botanic Garden, Edinburgh, 44(3). Article by Noble: *Beatrix Potter, Naturalist & Mycologist and Charles McIntosh, the 'Perthshire Naturalist'*. p. 616.
24. Taylor, Judy, Joyce Irene Whalley, Anne Stevenson Hobbs, and Elizabeth M. Battrick, *Beatrix Potter: The Artist and Her World*, p. 87.
25. Ramsbottom, John. 1922. *Journal of Botany*, Vol. 60, p. 188–9. Information kindly supplied by the Royal Botanic Society, Edinburgh.
26. Coates, op. cit., p. 238.

CHAPTER 12

Sir Henry Roscoe: Kew: Sir William Thiselton-Dyer

B EATRIX did much more than simply collect fungi and make illustrations of them. She studied every aspect of their life cycle in great detail. In fact, letters sent by her to Scotland to her mentor Charles McIntosh are akin to academic treatises, complete with all the terminology appropriate to the subject. 'The modern art student can draw ... but nobody seems to have [performed] the nature study ... behind the actual drawing', which she described as 'painstaking'.[1]

Her labours were not in vain, for she discovered ways in which fungi could be made to germinate from spores, the equivalent of seeds, something which was notoriously difficult to do. And having done so, she intended to bring her discovery to the attention of the highest authority (on botany) in the land, namely, William T. Thiselton-Dyer FRS CMG, member of the Athenaeum and Director of the Royal Botanic Gardens at Kew. Firstly, however, she would require a letter of introduction, and who better to provide it than her uncle, Professor of Chemistry and Fellow of the Royal Society, Sir Henry Enfield Roscoe of Woodcote in Surrey, the husband of her father's youngest sister, Lucy (who had married him in 1863); hence the entry in her journal, made on 27 February 1896, where she states confidently, 'Say I, he [Roscoe] will give me a note for Mr Thiselton-Dyer.'[2]

Although Beatrix was presently attempting to enlist her uncle's help, her comments about him had not always been of a charitable nature. For example, when, on 5 July 1884, she had learnt that he had been awarded a knighthood, she declared that she did not envy him, and added ungraciously:

> but how it makes us laugh ... there is very little doubt it is the successful result of always putting himself to the front and sticking to the Mundellas.[3] (A reference to Liberal politician, The Right Honourable Antony John Mundella, and his followers.)

Sir William Thiselton-Dyer graduated with a First Class Honours Degree from Christ Church College, Oxford. In 1868, he became Professor of Natural History at the Royal Agricultural College, Cirencester, and, two years later, Professor of Botany at the Royal College of Science, Dublin. In 1872 he was appointed Professor of Botany at the Royal Horticultural Society, London, a post he held until 1875.

Beatrix's first impression of the Director of Kew was:

> of a thin, elderly gentleman in summery attire [Thiselton-Dyer was, in fact, aged only fifty-two] with a dry, cynical manner, puffing a cigarette, but wide awake and boastful. He seemed pleased with my drawings, and a little surprised. He spoke kindly about the ticket [Beatrix had applied for a reader's ticket which would allow her access to Kew's library] and did not address me again, which I mention not with resentment, for I was getting dreadfully tired, but I had once or twice an amusing feeling of being regarded as young. [She was, in fact, aged twenty-two.]

For the remainder of the time the Director talked politics and discussed various matters relating to Kew with Roscoe, until the

impatient Beatrix 'shot in one remark which made him jump ...
[it was] as if they had forgotten my presence'. Finally, she
described Thiselton-Dyer as 'a Radical', not her favourite type
of person! 'I got home without collapse, a most interesting
morning,' said she, with thinly veiled sarcasm.[4]

Beatrix met Kew's director again on 7 December 1896. On this
occasion he was 'in a great hurry'.

> I was not shy, not at all. I had it up and down with
> him. His line was on the outside edge of civil, but I took
> it philosophically as a compliment to my appearance: he
> indicated that the subject was profound, that my opinions
> etc., 'mares nests' etc., that he hadn't time to look at my
> drawings, and referred me to the University of Cambridge. I
> informed him that it would be in all the books in ten years,
> whether or no, and departed giggling.

By 'mares nests', Thiselton-Dyer probably meant that Beatrix's
theories ('opinions') were matters of some complexity (although
the term can have a variety of meanings). But what was the
'it' which Beatrix referred to? A clue is to be found in a letter
which she wrote to Charles McIntosh, dated 12 January 1897, to
enquire:

> Have you ever suspected that there are *intermediate* species
> amongst Agarics and Boleti? We [herself and her uncle,
> Roscoe] are strongly of the opinion, for certain good reasons,
> that they are mixed fungi ... Of course such an idea is
> contrary to the books [i.e. to what was said in learned
> volumes on the subject], except for lichens ...

Whether Beatrix was right or wrong in her theories, complex
they certainly were!

Four days after her second meeting with Kew's Director, on
11 December, her Uncle Roscoe told her that he had received
a letter from Thiselton-Dyer which was both *rude* and *stupid.*'
He declined to show the letter to Beatrix, but told her that the

Director was 'a little rough-spoken and knew nothing about the subject ...' whereupon Beatrix declared, 'I imagine it contained advice that I should be sent to school because [or did Beatrix mean 'before'?] I began to teach other people.'[5]

Beatrix, in a sideswipe at Thiselton-Dyer, wrote in her journal on 26 December,

> We as outsiders express a pleasing, fresh irreverence for the leading botanical authorities, it really does seem very impertinent, but the things are there. It may just be that one sees them because one has an open mind, not in a groove.[6]

When Beatrix met with Thiselton-Dyer, it was in the hope that the value of her work would be recognized by 'the establishment', and that an account of it would appear in some learned journal. However, the response was not what she had hoped for and, instead, she felt that she was in the presence of an arrogant person who did not appreciate the importance of her mycological theories and discoveries. However, in fairness to Thiselton-Dyer, he had granted Beatrix an interview – two, in fact, despite his heavy workload and responsibilities. He was in charge of an organization of worldwide importance whose estimated number of staff ran into several hundred, with many more across the globe. Kew's director also did Beatrix the honour of admiring her drawings, and granted her a 'ticket' which would give her access to Kew's library and Herbarium.

Under Thiselton-Dyer's directorship, Kew, instead of being simply a repository of dead specimens of plants, was now a place where living plants were cultivated and studied, with the aim of disseminating botanic knowledge throughout the British Empire, for the benefit of both the mother countries, and the colonies. Had Beatrix's research had some practical application, or had she presented Kew's director with some new specimen of plant from India or from tropical Africa, the flora of which was of great interest to him personally, then he would surely have been enraptured.[7]

However, as Beatrix was not studying fungi for their nutritional or medicinal value, her studies fell entirely outside Kew's remit. Finally, although the director was a botanist, and a most eminent one, he was not a mycologist, and for this reason was not qualified to give a definitive opinion on Beatrix's findings. This is why he had referred her to Cambridge, to Henry Marshall Ward, the university's recently-appointed Professor of Botany (since 1895), who was eminent in the field of experimental botany and an expert in the particular field of mycology. Unfortunately, no record of Beatrix's interview with the professor exists, but there is reason to believe that he may have had an influence on future developments, as will now be seen.

Beatrix appears to have been intensely annoyed by Thiselton-Dyer's imperious and overbearing manner, as when, for example, according to her, he 'discoursed vaingloriously upon his Establishment'.[8] The last day of January 1896 saw her write in her journal that Thiselton-Dyer had 'snubbed' her.[9] The evidence, as presented above, however, does not support this view.

Notes

1. Beatrix to Sylvie Heelis, 17 September 1921. Taylor, *Beatrix Potter's Letters*, p. 273.
2. Linder, *The Journal of Beatrix Potter from 1881–1897*, 27 February 1896.
3. Ibid, 5 July 1884.
4. Linder, *The Journal of Beatrix Potter from 1881–1897*, 19 May 1896.
5. Ibid, 11 December 1896.
6. Ibid, 26 December 1896.
7. *Bulletin of Miscellaneous Information: Royal Botanic Gardens, Kew*, 1929, No. 3, p. 66.
8. Linder, op. cit., 19 May 1896.
9. Ibid, 31 January 1896.

CHAPTER 13

George Massee and the Linnean Society of London

O NE PERSON at Kew with whom Beatrix did manage to establish a good rapport was George Massee, Principal Assistant at the Herbarium. And on a second visit to Kew, which she made on 13 June 1896, her favourable impression of him was confirmed.

> I can only remark that it is much more interesting to talk to a person with ideas, even if they are not founded on very sufficient evidence.

Nevertheless, she had an in-depth conversation with him about some fungi which he was cultivating.[1] But when she returned to Kew on 18 November, she found herself disagreeing with Massee over a matter which, in her opinion, he 'knew very little about. I am afraid I contradicted him badly', she said.

That December, having met Thiselton-Dyer for the second time, Beatrix proceeded to the Herbarium, where she discovered that Massee 'had come round [to her way of thinking] altogether and was prepared to believe my new-thing [presumably her success at germinating fungi], including Lichens'.[2] And on

6 January 1897 Beatrix was delighted to be able to report that Massee, apparently under her instruction, had 'grown one of my best moulds'![3]

It was said of Thiselton-Dyer that 'no detail in administration was too small to escape his notice',[4] and it is therefore inconceivable that he was ignorant of the fact that Beatrix was engaged in prolonged and detailed discussions with his Principal Assistant about her theories, and that the two were involved together in practical experiments relating to the germination of fungal spores. And yet, to his credit, he was prepared to tolerate this, when he might have forbidden it on the grounds that it was an unwelcome distraction to a key member of his staff, by an intruder who was an amateur with no academic qualifications.

Beatrix wrote jubilantly to Charles McIntosh on 22 February, on the subject of a scientific paper that she had written. 'I succeeded in sprouting the mushroom spore ...' (i.e. in germinating spores of the *Agaric* family of mushrooms.) However, 'it seems that no one else is admitted [acknowledged] to have done it', and because of this fact, she feared that 'No one except my uncle [Roscoe] & one gentleman at Kew [i.e. George Massee] will believe that any of my [microscopic] slides are right.' She then proceeded to tell McIntosh that she had grown:

> between 40 & 50 sorts of [fungal] spore, but I think we shall probably only send in A. [Agaricus] velutipes, which I have grown on [i.e. propagated] twice and Mr Massee has also grown according to my direction at Kew. He did not previously believe in the things at all. I am just as much sure of the mushroom but unless I can get a good slide [of the spore] actually sprouting it seems useless to send it to the Linnean.[5]

Massee, in his efforts to assist Beatrix, went even further, when, at a meeting of the prestigious Linnean Society of London (founded in 1788 to promote all aspects of the biological sciences, of which Massee was himself a member), held on 1 April 1897 under the presidency of Dr A. Günther FRS, he himself

'Communicated' [i.e. presumably read aloud] her paper 'On the Germination of the Spores of *Agaricineae*' by Miss Helen B. Potter to the assembled company.[6] Massee may have suggested this of his own volition, or the idea may have come either from her Uncle Roscoe, whose paternal grandfather, William, had been a friend of Sir James Edward Smith, the Linnean Society's founder and first president, or from Professor Ward, who was also a fellow of the society.

For Beatrix, this was a tremendous honour and accolade, and she was surely aware that she was following in the footsteps of none other than Charles Darwin and Alfred Russel Wallace, whose papers on the burning topic of the day – evolution – had been presented to the Linnean Society almost four decades previously, on 1 July 1858. As a woman, however, she was debarred from attending the meeting at which her paper was presented. Nevertheless, papers written by women were sometimes published in both the *Transactions* of the society and in its *Journal*, which was undoubtedly what she had hoped for.

At that very same meeting, it is reported that four other people either exhibited artefacts or presented papers, one of them being none other than Kew's director, Mr W. T. Thiselton-Dyer himself, who displayed (i) A series of drawings (on the screen) to illustrate the 'cultural evolution of cyclamen latifolum Sibth.' This species is a native of Greece and the Levant ... (ii) A series of plants was exhibited to illustrate the origin of the garden 'Cineraria' ...[7]

The others were George R. M. Murray, Keeper of the Department of Botany at the Natural History Museum (and an acquaintance of Beatrix); Alfred W. Bennett, Lecturer in Botany at St Thomas's Hospital (the study of Botany was part of the syllabus for medical students in those days, plants being the principal source of medicinal products), and another botanist, Henry Groves. The fact that Thiselton-Dyer was actually present when Beatrix's paper was read out is a further indication that the former was fully cognizant of the association between herself and Massee.

However, only one week after the reading of the paper, it was recorded in the Minutes of the Council of the Linnean Society that 'A proposal on behalf of Miss Helen [Beatrix] Potter to withdraw her paper 'On the germination of spores of *Agaricineae*, No. 2978' had been sanctioned.[8] In other words, it would not be considered for publication (for reasons indicated below). The following day, however, Beatrix indicated in her journal that she still entertained hopes that her ideas about fungi might be published, possibly by George Massee, of whom she said:

> I do not in the least suspect that mild gentleman of any design of poaching ... but if he casually put them [her ideas] into his books I should wish to have an acknowledgment.[9]

Beatrix made a further reference to her scientific paper in a letter to Charles McIntosh, dated 21 September 1897, in which she stated that it had been:

> 'well received' according to Mr Massee, but they [presumably the powers-that-be at the Linnean Society] say it requires more work on it before it is printed.[10]

This, presumably, was why Beatrix had withdrawn the paper (the present whereabouts of which are unknown). But why did she not resubmit it? Was this because she lacked the scientific knowledge, or the technical expertise to do the 'extra work on it' that was evidently required? But surely, if this was the case, then Massee would have helped her with it. Or was it simply because she had tired of the project? Of the two, the latter proposition would seem the more likely.

Despite her best efforts, Beatrix had failed to obtain the academic recognition for her work which she felt she deserved. She tried to make light of the experience, but it must have come as a bitter blow. (However, seven decades later, in 1967, Dr Walter P. K. Findlay, a former President of the British Mycological Society, considered her watercolour paintings of fungi to be of such high quality that he included fifty-nine of them in his book *Wayside and Woodland Fungi*, published by Frederick Warne. And a further three decades later, on 24 April 1997, Professor Roy Watling of the Royal Botanic Gardens, Edinburgh, gave recognition to her research in a lecture to the Linnean Society entitled 'Beatrix Potter as Mycologist'. Not surprisingly, Beatrix's interest in mycology waned from then on, as did her correspondence with Charles McIntosh. However, she continued to make the occasional paintings of fungi.

* * *

The failure of Beatrix to achieve her ambition, the publication of her paper either by the Linnean Society, or elsewhere, and the widespread recognition of the importance of her work that this would have afforded her, must be seen in the context of the times, and in the light of the fact that she was a woman.

In Victorian times the children of wealthy, middle-class parents were educated along similar lines by their governesses until they reached the age of seven. The son would then proceed to preparatory school, followed, at the age of eleven to thirteen, by public school (where Latin, Greek, and mathematics formed a substantial part of the curriculum) and, finally, university. For the daughter, it was different. She continued to be taught by her governess in a dedicated room of her home, set aside to serve as a schoolroom where:

> The genteel female curriculum emphasized French and German or Italian, music, history, watercolour sketching, and the kind of basic cultural knowledge that would fit young women to listen intelligently to their future husbands.[11]

Beatrix, as a passionate devotee of natural history and natural science, did not fit into this stereotypical pattern, but she was fortunate in having parents who tolerated her hobby, and a father who positively encouraged it. However, she was disadvantaged in having no formal academic training or qualifications. (As she herself said, Thiselton-Dyer may have alluded to this fact in his letter to her Uncle Roscoe.) And just how much of a disadvantage this was became clear at the Linnean Society, when it was suggested to her that her scientific paper required more work.

In respect of learning, Beatrix was an individualist who, though she was always anxious to learn, did not always like being taught. As she declared in later life:

> Thank goodness, my education was neglected; I was never sent to school. The reason I am glad I did not go to school; it would have rubbed off some of the originality (if I had not died of shyness or been killed of over pressure).[12]

In other words, Beatrix felt that schooling would have blunted the originality of her thinking. However, by the time she came to write these words, she had achieved worldwide success in a quite different sphere of activity, as will shortly be seen. Had she not achieved this success then perhaps her attitude to further education would have been different. (One possible reason why the Potters chose not to send Beatrix to school was that Mrs Potter was afraid that her daughter would catch 'germs'. This was also the reason, as will be seen, why Mrs Potter discouraged her daughter from having childhood friends.)

Despite her disappointment, the fires of creativity continued to burn brightly within Beatrix, and the question was, in which direction would her creative instincts now take her?

Notes

1. Linder, *The Journal of Beatrix Potter from 1881–1897*, 13 June 1896.
2. Ibid, 7 December 1896.
3. Ibid, 6 January 1897.
4. *Bulletin of Miscellaneous Information: Royal Botanic Gardens, Kew*, 1929. No. 3. p. 65.
5. Beatrix to Charles McIntosh, 22 February 1897. Coppins, B. J. (editor). 1987. Notes from the Royal Botanic Garden, Edinburgh, 44(3). Article by Noble: *Beatrix Potter, Naturalist & Mycologist and Charles McIntosh, the 'Perthshire Naturalist'*. pp. 607–27.

6. *Proceedings of the Linnean Society*, 1 April 1897.
7. Ibid.
8. Council Minutes of the Linnean Society, 8 April 1897.
9. Linder, op. cit., 9 January 1897.
10. Beatrix to Charles McIntosh, 21 September 1897. Coppins, B. J. (editor). 1987. Notes from the Royal Botanic Garden, Edinburgh, 44(3). Article by Noble: *Beatrix Potter, Naturalist & Mycologist and Charles McIntosh, the 'Perthshire Naturalist'*. pp. 607–27.
11. Nelson, *Family Ties in Victorian England*, p. 78.
12. 'Roots of the Peter Rabbit Tales'. *The Horn Book*. May 1929.

CHAPTER 14

Art: Anthropomorphism:
First Encounters with
Publishers

BEATRIX was a person whose interests included such subjects as music, art, literature, and science. This was fortunate for her because had she limited herself to natural science only, then, following the demise of her scientific paper on the germination of fungal spores, she would have had no other outlet for her creative energies.

Beatrix enjoyed reading books which contained illustrations, for example those by Scottish children's writer Mary Louise Molesworth which she collected as soon as they were published.[1] However, for her, it was two male illustrators who stole the limelight.

Walter Crane (1845–1915) was the son of Thomas Crane, portrait painter and miniaturist, and Beatrix possessed a work by him with a particularly long title, *The Baby's Opera: a Book of Old Nursery Rhymes in New Verses: The Music by the Earliest Masters*. As the title indicates, neither the music nor the poetry was by Crane, only the illustrations. Here, each poem is illustrated with figures of both human beings and animals. Generally, the animals appear *au naturel*, i.e. unclothed, but in his illustration of the poem 'Ye Frog's Wooing' the frog is wearing a hat, boots and a cummerbund, the rat, trousers and overcoat, the mouse, a dress and frilly bonnet. A possible criticism might be that his portraits are somewhat stylized and two-dimensional.

Randolph Caldecott (1846–86) was the son of a Chester businessman and accountant who began his career by working in a bank. He subsequently became an illustrator of traditional folk and fairy tales, fables, and nursery rhymes, and it was his work which was to make the greatest impression on Beatrix, as far as her own future endeavours were concerned. And not only that, the Potters would come to possess some of Caldecott's original art work, for, as Beatrix stated, in February 1884:

> Papa went to the Fine Arts Gallery and bought two small pen-and-ink sketches from Caldecott's *Frog*. [This was a reference to sketches which Caldecott had made to illustrate his children's book, *A Frog He Would A-Wooing Go*, in which the rhymes derive from a 16th-century poem entitled 'The Frog Came to the Myl Dur' (Mill Door), which appeared in *The Complaynt of Scotland*, published in 1548]. He wanted to buy the last coloured sketch from *The Fox* [A reference to *The Fox Jumps over the Parson's Gate*, which was also illustrated by Caldecott] but they would not sell it separately. They wanted £10 more now than when Papa bought the other set of *The Three Huntsmen* by Caldecott, for £80.

These titles were part of a set of sixteen 'picture books' which were published annually, in pairs, from 1878 until Caldecott's death in 1886, and always in time for Christmas. The lot which Mr Potter purchased included eight of Caldecott's illustrations for *The Three Jovial Huntsmen*, a traditional poem in the Lancashire dialect.[2] Mr Potter's collection of Caldecott's works also included:

> a frame of coloured designs for '[The] Curmudgeon's Christmas' which appeared in *The Graphic* [in December

1885], and 4 Brittany Folk and most of the pen & inks of the Mad Dog [*Elegy on the Death of a Mad Dog* was a poem by Anglo-Irish playwright, novelist, and poet Oliver Goldsmith] ...[3]

Of Caldecott, Beatrix declared:

> We bought his picture books eagerly as they came out. I have the greatest admiration for his work – a jealous appreciation; for I think that others, whose names are commonly bracketed with his, are not in the same plane at all as artist/illustrators. For instance, Kate Greenaway's pictures are very charming, but compared with Caldecott, she could not draw. [Greenaway was a children's writer and illustrator, whose book of pictures and nursery rhymes entitled *Under the Window*, also featured in Beatrix' collection.] Others who followed him were careful & correct draughts-men but lifeless and wooden. Besides; Walter Crane and Caldecott were the pioneers; their successors were imitators only.[4]

For Beatrix the appeal of Caldecott was that his animals, both wild and domestic, were attired in human-type clothes, used human-type implements and spoke English (even though they engaged in animal-like activities). For example, in *A Frog He Would A-Wooing Go*, the frog sits drinking tea with a male and female rat, and appears to be tempting the male rat into an animated conversation, their human-style clothes and shoes being painted in subtle, pastel colours. This technique of Caldecott, the attribution of human characteristics to animals, is known as anthropomorphism. (Humans also appear in *A Frog He Would A-wooing Go*, but in a purely passive role.) There is no doubt, in view of what was to follow in terms of Beatrix's own development as an artist/illustrator, that Caldecott's works had an influence above all others.

When Beatrix looked about her for a creature to paint or draw she did not have to look far for, as author Judy Taylor points out, she and her brother Bertram, both as children and as adults, possessed many living creatures, which, in Beatrix's case, numbered over the years, in excess of ninety, 'not including the snails'. Of these, there was a great variety, including:

> lizards, dogs, cats, horses, cocks and hens, guinea pigs and ordinary pigs, sheep, squirrels, mice and dormice, rats, frogs and toads, newts, salamanders, cows, a kestrel, a parrot, a ring snake and bats. To every one they gave a name, and Beatrix drew or painted most of them.[5]

Some of these pets lived in the schoolroom at 2 Bolton Gardens as a sketch of it by Beatrix, in which she depicts caged birds and a tortoise peering through the fireguard, indicates.[6] Others, presumably, were kept in the garden.

As already mentioned Beatrix regarded all her creatures as pets, companions even. She took a great interest in their daily lives, studied their habits and their personalities, and was bitterly disappointed when any of them fell ill or died. For example, on 18 October 1886, she noted in her journal the demise of '*poor Miss Mouse*, otherwise [known as] *Xarifa* [and declared] I was very much distressed . . .'.[7] But there was more to it than this. With her powers of intuition she could, in the case of her more intelligent pets, read their minds, comprehend their thoughts, and even imagine them conversing with one another when they interacted. So, with her artistic ability, what more natural than that she should wish to depict them by sketch or watercolour?

Rabbits appear in Beatrix's second sketchbook of 1876, created by her when she was aged nine. She would always keep rabbits as pets, and author Judy Taylor has discovered the names of ten (and there were probably more) which she owned during her lifetime. In this sketchbook she portrays animals engaged in a variety of human-style pursuits, such as going for a walk on a windy day, or sledging in the snow. What is more, many of these animals, particularly the rabbits, are wearing human-type clothes, the inspiration for this being, undoubtedly, the works of Caldecott and Crane. Beatrix also enjoyed copying the work of other artists (as did her brother Bertram). For example, in her 1876 sketchbook in an illustration of hers, which is derived from Jemima Blackburn's children's book *The Pipits*, mice are depicted running up and down a pendulum clock and stealing fruit and cheese.[8]

Despite the difference of almost six years in age between Beatrix and her younger brother Bertram, the two often collaborated with each other on various projects, one of these being the production, in 1889, of homemade Christmas cards for the family. However, when, at the appropriate time they duly placed the cards on the breakfast table, each one under its appropriate plate, their kind and thoughtful gesture was met with little enthusiasm, and all that remained for them to do was to comfort one another. Said Beatrix of herself and her brother, 'we work a mutual admiration society and go *in moaning* together over the apathy of the rest of the family.' One of the recipients of the cards was Uncle Roscoe, who *did* offer a word of encouragement. Any publisher, he declared, 'would snap at them [i.e. be eager to publish the cards which they had produced]'.

At first, Beatrix entertained the idea of printing the cards herself but was deterred by the fact that the cost of a printing machine was £16. She would, therefore, design six different cards, each featuring her pet rabbit 'Benjamin' (otherwise known as 'Benjamin Bouncer', 'Benjamin Bunny', or 'Bounce'; he was in fact a hare), and attempt to get them published. And in this the odds were in her favour, for although the proprietors of publishing houses were predominantly male, several female book illustrators of the highest order had already made their mark on the publishing world.

By Easter 1890 the designs for six cards were duly completed. However, her pet was not entirely co-operative. 'I was rather impeded ... by ... the idiosyncrasies of Benjamin who has an appetite for certain sorts of paint, but the cards were finished by Easter ...' [9] In one of the illustrations, Beatrix depicts a rabbit couple talking animatedly as they trudge through the snow. One is attired in a purple coat and is holding a basket, the other is attired in an orange bonnet and green skirt and is holding what appears to be a bunch of mistletoe.

Beatrix sent her designs to five publishers, including Marcus Ward & Sons of Belfast, and Raphael Tuck, without success. Her brother Bertram now suggested that she try German publishers Hildesheimer & Faulkner of Manchester, who also had a branch at 41 Jewin Street, London. He would deliver the items personally, as he set off on his way to Oxford in order to sit that university's entrance examination. This time Beatrix was successful. She received a cheque for £6 for her labours and a request for more of her work.[10] Beatrix, accompanied by her uncle (presumably Roscoe), duly delivered the extra sketches to Mr Faulkner, in person, at his London office.

> He was very civil to me, but so dry and circumspect in the way of business that I cannot think of him without laughing. Not one word did he say in praise of the cards, but he showed a mysterious desire for more.[11]

Beatrix, however, soon discovered that her tastes and those of Faulkner were, in some respects, poles apart. For example, his 'peculiar fondness' for depictions of 'little men with cats' heads stuck on their shoulders' was not shared by Beatrix. Nor did she share his liking for 'fiddles [i.e. violins] and trousers', presumably to be played and worn respectively by anthropomorphically depicted creatures. And neither did she accede to his request that she paint certain animals of his liking. For, in her words, 'it was the humour that signified, not the likeness.' This comment by Beatrix is highly significant. For her there was no merit in painting animals unless she found them entertaining. Had Faulkner shared her view, then a highly successful collaboration may well have resulted.

As it was Beatrix's designs were used by Hildesheimer & Faulkner to illustrate Christmas and New Year cards. The illustrations also appeared, in combination with poetical verses by lawyer, author, radio entertainer, and songwriter Frederick

Edward Weatherly (whose greatest claim to fame is the composition of the ballad Danny Boy, to the tune of 'An Irish Air from the County Londonderry'), in a small volume entitled *A Happy Pair*. Published in 1893, it sold for 4½d (fourpence halfpenny, or less than 2p) whereupon

> my first act was to give Bounce [Benjamin] (what an investment that rabbit has been in spite of the [expense of] hutches), a cupful of hemp seeds, the consequence being that when I wanted to draw him next morning he was partially intoxicated and wholly unmanageable.[12]

In 1892 Beatrix's drawing of a jackdaw, comically holding a set of chimney sweep's brushes under its wing, was accepted by Ernest Nister & Co. of London, a German company of fine art printers and publishers of children's books and annuals. Further successes followed. In May 1894 Beatrix sent Ernest Nister & Co. nine of her drawings of frogs. When the company made her an offer for them, which she considered to be inadequate, she had no hesitation in standing up for herself. Unless Nister & Co. was willing to pay the price which she was asking, then she must trouble them to return the drawings.[13] In the event, Nister increased its offer and paid her the asking price of twenty-two shillings and sixpence (£1.2½p). The drawings were subsequently used by them to illustrate a booklet of theirs entitled *A Frog He Would A-Fishing Go*. (Some of Beatrix's drawings subsequently appeared in *Nister's Holiday Annual for 1896*.)

Sometimes Beatrix was inspired to produce illustrations for books which she had read, as, for example, when John Bright, who occasionally visited the Potters in the Lake District, introduced her to US writer Joel Chandler Harris's 'Uncle Remus' fables which were based on African-American folklore. So appealing did she find these fables that, between 1893 and 1896, she produced eight illustrations based on *Uncle Remus: His Songs and Sayings* (published in 1880, as the first of ten volumes), and on *Nights with Uncle Remus* (1883). Here, once again, rabbits were the centre of attraction, namely Harris's trickster 'Br'er Rabbit' and his friend 'Br'er Fox'. Other rabbits featured around the border of each of Beatrix's portraits. Similarly, in 1893, for Lewis Carroll's *Alice's Adventures in Wonderland* (published in 1865), she produced illustrations in which she attired Carroll's fictional character, the White Rabbit, in a purple coat and pink waistcoat.

Under the tutelage of Miss Cameron, the unidentified 'Mrs A' and, to a lesser extent Sir John Millais, Beatrix had become a qualified and highly competent artist. Soon, through her anthropomorphic art, and with the co-operation of another pet rabbit called 'Peter' (Benjamin having died some time prior to the spring of 1893), she would not only gain the recognition which she deserved but would also become famous throughout the world.

Notes

1. Beatrix to Helen Dean Fish, 8 December 1934. Taylor, *Beatrix Potter's Letters*, p. 369.
2. Linder, *The Journal of Beatrix Potter from 1881–1897*, 8 February 1884.
3. Beatrix to Jacqueline Overton. 7 April 1942. Taylor, *Beatrix Potter's Letters*, p. 442.
4. Beatrix to Jacqueline Overton, 7 April 1942. Taylor, *Beatrix Potter's Letters*, p. 441.
5. Taylor, *An Affectionate Companion and a Quiet Friend: Beatrix's Pets as a Source of her Inspiration*. Beatrix Potter Studies XII. pp. 74–5.
6. Sketch by Beatrix, made on 26 November 1885 in Journal, 1966 edition, facing p. 168.
7. Linder, op. cit., December 1886.
8. Taylor, Judy, Joyce Irene Whalley, Anne Stevenson Hobbs, and Elizabeth M. Battrick, *Beatrix Potter: The Artist and Her World*, p. 39.
9. Linder, op. cit., May 1890.
10. Ibid.
11. Ibid.
12. Ibid.
13. Beatrix to E. Nister, 2 June 1894. Judy Taylor, *Beatrix Potter's Letters*, p. 28.

CHAPTER 15

Noel Moore and the 'Picture Letter'

A S A CHILD, Beatrix had existed in a world almost totally devoid of childhood playmates and, in consequence, she never learned to relate to them on a personal level. And when she became an adult she preferred to communicate with children by letter, rather than to meet them face to face.

Beatrix was a diligent correspondent whose habit it was, when writing to children, to incorporate into her letters amusing stories which she illustrated with sketches. It was on 11 March 1892, when she was aged twenty-five, that she sent such a letter to four-year-old Noel, eldest son of her former governess, Annie Moore. This 'picture letter' (an expression coined by Beatrix herself), which was written from the Falmouth Hotel, Falmouth, Cornwall, was illustrated prolifically, with railway locomotive and carriages, people promenading beneath palm trees in a garden of shrubs, a steamboat and a fisherman catching crabs from a rowing boat, together with a collection of sailing boats, a cat, dogs, ducks and chickens. However, it was Beatrix's second letter to Noel, of 4 September 1893, written from Eastwood House, Dunkeld, Perthshire and featuring the fictional character

'Peter' (Rabbit) which would become the most famous picture letter of all time. The letter began:

> My dear Noel, I don't know what to write to you, so I shall tell you a story about four little rabbits whose names were – Flopsy, Mopsy, Cottontail and Peter.

The letter was illustrated with pictures of 'Old Mrs Bunny', and of her offspring Flopsy, Mopsy, Cottontail and, finally, Peter, the principal character and villain of the piece who was 'very naughty'. Mrs Bunny has strictly forbidden her young bunnies to venture into the garden of a certain Mr McGregor but, of course, Peter does, and there is a picture of Mr McGregor angrily shooing him away with a garden fork, but only after Peter has devoured a quantity of lettuces, broad beans and radishes! What is particularly significant about this letter is that Mrs Bunny is depicted wearing a dress and apron, her daughters little capes, and Peter a jacket. Also, the rabbits engage in human-like pursuits as they collect raspberries in a basket and eat bread and drink milk. And when Peter is ill his mother doses him with camomile tea.

This letter contained no fewer than thirty images of rabbits, principally Peter. The name of 'Peter Rabbit' and of his creator, Beatrix Potter, would become famous throughout the world. Beatrix wrote many subsequent letters, of which at least twenty-six survive, to Noel, who at the age of nine suffered an attack of poliomyelitis which left him with a permanent limp. She also wrote letters to his siblings, of which thirteen were sent to Eric, ten to Winifrede, five to Marjorie and one to Norah. The Moore children, who treasured Beatrix's letters, kept them all, which, as it transpired, proved to be providential.

In the spring of 1900 Beatrix enquired as to whether she might be permitted to borrow some of the picture letters which she had sent over the years to the Moore children. Her wish was granted, and she proceeded to make a copy of the 'Peter Rabbit' letter which she had written to Noel in 1893. She increased the amount of text and added some new illustrations, in black and white. She also painted a frontispiece in colour, depicting Mrs Rabbit administering camomile tea to Peter. She then sent her manuscript, now entitled *The Tale of Peter Rabbit and Mr McGregor's Garden*, to half a dozen or so publishers, including Frederick Warne & Co (who, as she would undoubtedly have been aware, had already published books by some of her favourite authors and illustrators, including Walter Crane, Kate Greenaway, Edward Lear and Randolph Caldecott). Astonishingly, all of them rejected it. She therefore decided to have it printed privately, by Strangeway & Sons of Tower Street, London, who, in December 1901, produced 250 copies in which all the illustrations, with the exception of the frontispiece, were in black and white. (In February 1902 there was a second, private, printing of 200 copies.) It was now that another male friend of the family, forty-nine-year-old the Reverend Hardwicke Drummond Rawnsley, took Beatrix under his wing and lent a hand on her behalf.

On hearing of Beatrix's disappointment over her Peter Rabbit book, Rawnsley took it upon himself, as a published author, to convert the narrative of the story into rhyme and, in the autumn of 1901, at his behest, Beatrix sent the first part of the manuscript back to Frederick Warne in order that they might reconsider it. This time, and possibly because the success of Beatrix's privately-printed editions had come to their notice, Warne's response was more positive. However, the publishers decided that they preferred the original form, and therefore asked for Rawnsley's rhymes to be converted back to 'simple narration'. They also required that all the illustrations be in colour. Meanwhile, in February 1902, Beatrix had another 200 copies printed privately.

When Beatrix was about to commence work on recreating the Peter Rabbit illustrations in colour, there came a setback. Said she:

> Peter [her real-life rabbit] died, at 9 years old, just before I began the drawings, & now when they are finished I have got another young rabbit, & the drawings look wrong.[1]

She was a perfectionist, and this failure of hers to live up to the high standards which she had set for herself would have perplexed her exceedingly. Nonetheless, the problem was finally overcome and, in October 1902, *The Tale of Peter Rabbit* was published by Warne.

In *The Tale of Peter Rabbit* the scene of the action is Mr McGregor's garden where Peter, having illicitly devoured a quantity of vegetables, is hotly pursued by the owner. Could it be that Arthur Melville's painting 'Cabbage Garden', mentioned previously, was the inspiration for Beatrix's 'Mr McGregor's Garden'? Although it has to be said that lettuce would have been more to 'Peter' rabbit's taste than cabbages.

The Tale of Peter Rabbit was an immediate and astounding success, with 28,220 copies being produced (in three printings) during the first year alone. Could Beatrix have imagined that this was just the beginning?

* * *

The Tailor of Gloucester was the second of Beatrix's 'tales', although it was the third to be published by Warne. It, too, is based on a picture letter dated 'Christmas 1901' which Beatrix composed for Winifrede, another of Annie Moore's children. Winifrede (whom Beatrix addressed as 'Freda') had recently been unwell and Beatrix hoped that her letter would entertain her and cheer her up. It concerns a tailor who leaves cut-out templates, intended for a waistcoat, in his shop over the week-end, only to return to work, the following Monday, to find it completed – with the sole exception of one buttonhole. On a piece of paper pinned to the garment are written the words 'no more twist' (i.e. the mysterious maker had run out of thread). Declared Beatrix to Winifrede:

> And the queerest thing about it – is that I heard it in Gloucestershire and it is true! at least about the tailor, the waistcoat, and the 'no more twist'.[2]

According to Beatrix, she:

> had [heard] the story from [her cousin] Miss Caroline Hutton, who had it of Miss Lucy, of Gloucester, who had it of the tailor [i.e. a real tailor of Gloucester].[3]

Fortunately, Winifrede had kept the letter and in due course Beatrix was able to borrow it and make use of it in the writing of *The Tailor of Gloucester*. Here, once again, we see little creatures (this time appearing *au naturel*) engaged in human-type pursuits: mice enjoying sewing and embroidery, and the household cat, Simpkin, being sent on an errand by the tailor to purchase bread, milk and sausages. Over the succeeding years, Beatrix would produce another twenty-two such 'tales', all to be published by Warne, and all of which became highly popular and successful.

Beatrix's 'tales' served not only to entertain and amuse, but their creation also served as a mental therapy to their author, for as Lady Ulla Hyde Parker so discerningly points out:

> Cousin Beatie [Beatrix] was aware of the great talent that she had been given, and from the loneliness she had felt, from the disappointments and hurts life had inflicted on her, she had understood how to draw out the light which lies at the centre of each dark experience, however distressing, and also how to retain her true self. She had retreated into a simple life close to nature, and in that life she had seen, and drawn for others to see, the pure loveliness of a rabbit, a frog, a hedgehog, mice and other small animals; she gave them a personality and made them live. A hole in the wall with mice, the surface of a lake or pond with reeds and the broad leaves of water-lilies became miniature worlds ...[4]

But did Ulla's analysis of events tell the whole story? This remains to be seen.

Notes

1. Beatrix to F. Warne & Co., 8 May 1902. Taylor, *Beatrix Potter's Letters*, p. 62.
2. Beatrix to Winifrede Moore, Christmas 1901. Linder, *A History of the Writings of Beatrix Potter*, p. 113.
3. Ibid, p. 111.
4. Hyde Parker, *Cousin Beatie: a Memory of Beatrix Potter*, p. 27.

CHAPTER 16

Norman Warne

IT WAS NOT until 1901, when she was aged thirty-five, that Beatrix fell seriously in love, and when she did it was with thirty-three-year-old Norman Dalziel Warne, who was junior partner in the firm Frederick Warne & Co., publishers of her illustrated children's stories. Seven years previously she had declared, 'I hold an old-fashioned notion that a happy marriage is the crown of a woman's life ...'[1] And now, it seemed, her chance had come.

It was in this way that the romance came about. On 11 September 1901 Beatrix had written to Messrs Warne & Co. from Lingholm in the Lake District in connection with her 'Peter Rabbit' book. Having returned home to London a week before Christmas, she wrote to Warne again to say, 'I should be glad to call some time at the office to hear what you decide about the coloured drawings.' It is likely, therefore, that Beatrix first met Norman at Christmastime in that year.

Norman's father was Frederick Warne who, in 1865, had started a publishing firm, the address of which was Chandos Building, Bedford Street, Strand, London. His mother was Louisa Jane (née Fruing) from the Channel Island of Jersey; her family owned a fishing company. Norman was the couple's youngest child.

When Norman was born on 6 July 1868 he already had six surviving siblings: Edith (aged fifteen); Frederick William (fourteen); Amelia Louise ('Millie' ten); Harold Edmund (eight); (William) Fruing (seven), and Edwin Lewis (two-and-a-half). Edwin, however, died only five months later, as did Frederick William, two years later, in 1870. Having completed their schooling, Harold, Fruing and Norman joined their father Frederick's firm. On 25 May 1895, Frederick (then in partnership with one Edward James Dodd) dissolved his partnership and retired. His three sons would now carry on the business under the name of Frederick Warne & Co.: Harold as Managing Director; Fruing as Sales Manager, and Norman as Production Manager and Travelling Salesman. Frederick died on 7 November 1901.

When Beatrix first met Norman he was living with his widowed mother, Louisa, and his unmarried sister, Millie (who was eight years older than Beatrix), in Bedford Square, Bloomsbury, his two elder brothers having married and left home. Both of them also lived in London, Harold at Surbiton, and Fruing at Primrose Hill.

Norman, who was fond of cycling and tennis, is described as the 'favourite uncle' of his brother and sister's children:

> He it was who uncomplainingly assumed the red robes and hood and flowing white beard at Christmas parties, speaking through the whiskers in a muffled voice and pretending to be immensely put out when one of his nieces recognized him in spite of all, and ran up and kissed him in the midst of it because it was 'only Uncle Norman.' His was the magic lantern which beguiled them on winter evenings after tea ...[2]

Beatrix wrote to Norman on 30 April 1902, addressing him formally as 'Mr Warne', in accordance with the custom of the times, and offering to redraw two of the pictures of Peter Rabbit for the proposed *Tale of Peter Rabbit*.[3] Three weeks later she told

Norman that she regretted not having called to see him but was unable to leave Mrs Potter who had suffered an attack of influenza. She also entreated Norman that if her father, Mr Potter, a qualified barrister, insisted on accompanying her to view the publishing agreement between herself and Frederick Warne & Co., then would he [Norman] 'please not mind him very much, if he is fidgety about things ...? I think it is better to mention beforehand he is sometimes a little difficult ... I can of course do what I like about the book being [aged] thirty-six.' In other words, whatever her father's opinion might be, Beatrix would have the final say.[4]

Beatrix informed Norman on 15 July that she and the family were about to go on holiday for three months, as was their custom. Was it possible, she wondered, that Warne might like to publish another of her stories? 'I did not mean to ask you to say you would take another book,' said she, diffidently to Norman, but she intended to write another one 'in any event because I want something to do ...'. Meanwhile, fearing that Warne would be unlikely to accept a second book so quickly after the first, Beatrix arranged to have 500 copies of *The Tailor of Gloucester* printed privately, in December 1902. However, she need not have worried, for her wishes were granted and, in early 1903, the company agreed to publish not one, but two more of her books: *The Tailor of Gloucester* and *The Tale of Squirrel Nutkin*.

Beatrix was involved not only with the writing and illustrating of her books, but in prolific and detailed correspondence about them with Norman. She discussed the style of binding, punctuation, grammar, number of pictures and number of words to be included, layout, etc. And she was not averse to criticizing the proofs of her work if she considered them to be unsatisfactory. For example, in regard to *The Tale of Squirrel Nutkin* she said, 'I notice one page of proofs is *all* too green, another *all* too red etc., so I think it is clearly the printer's fault.'[5]

Beatrix told Norman on 20 March 1903 that she was anxious to proceed with shortening the narrative of *The Tailor of Gloucester*, a task which she felt she must begin before Easter because then 'I have to go away for a fortnight always [i.e. as is customary] with my parents.' She also told him, on 13 April, that a drawing, by her, of the 'oldfashioned fireplace' at Melford Hall, the home of her cousin Ethel, Lady Hyde Parker, would serve most admirably to include as an illustration for *The Tailor of Gloucester*'s kitchen. By 8 July an uncharacteristically diffident Beatrix had plucked up the courage to tell Norman:

> I had been a little hoping ... that something might be said about another book, but I did not know that I was the right person to make that suggestion! I could send you a list to consider. There are plenty in a vague state of existence ...

Five days later, Beatrix, who was shortly to travel to the Lake District for the Potter family's customary holiday, told Harold Warne, Norman's elder brother, that she regretted that she:

> cannot call again at the office before leaving town. And I should not have mentioned the subject of another book at present. I have had such painful unpleasantness at home this winter about the work that I should like a rest while I am away. I should be obliged if you would kindly say no more about a new book at present.

From these remarks it may be inferred that one or other of Beatrix's parents, and possibly both, were putting obstacles in the path of her writing, probably because they objected to her association with Norman Warne.

Beatrix wrote to Norman on 20 August 1903 from Fawe Park, Derwentwater near Keswick in the Lake District, to tell him that she was delighted about the success of 'Nutkin', *The Tale of Squirrel Nutkin* which was published in that same month.[6] The following month, writing again from Fawe Park, she told Norman that to spend 'three months away from home is always more than enough ...'. Nevertheless, she had not been idle and had 'done every imaginable rabbit background, & miscellaneous sketches as well – about 70.' This was for *The Tale of Benjamin Bunny* which Warne had also agreed to publish.[7]

In December 1903, with a view to enlarging the range of her merchandizable products, Beatrix was busy making a Peter Rabbit doll, the design of which she proceeded to patent. And having done so, she sent the doll to Norman to give to one of his nieces. She subsequently discussed with Norman a proposal for wallpapers, designed for children's nurseries, which would be produced by Arthur Sanderson & Sons of Berners Street, London and feature the characters in her books.[8]

Beatrix then had the notion of writing a story about two mice. But first it was necessary for her to provide suitable accommodation for two, real-life pet mice which she had rescued from the cage-trap in which they had been caught in the kitchen of Harescombe Grange, the Gloucestershire home of her Hutton cousins Caroline and Mary.

Knowing that 'Johnny Crow', a nickname originally given to Uncle Norman by his nephews and nieces, and subsequently adopted by Beatrix,[9] was something of an amateur carpenter, Beatrix asked him if he would kindly construct 'a little house' for these pet mice of hers. This he did, complete with glass front, to enable Beatrix to observe the mice whilst she was sketching them.[10] Beatrix named her male mouse 'Tom Thumb' and his wife 'Hunca Munca'.[11] They would shortly appear with names unchanged in *The Tale of Two Bad Mice*.

In the story dolls Lucinda and Jane were to inhabit a doll's house and it so happened that Norman had already made such an object for Winifred, daughter of his brother, Fruing, a three-storey replica of an Edwardian villa, complete with interior furnishings. He therefore suggested to Beatrix that she might like to visit Fruing's house in Surbiton to make a sketch of it. However, this was not as straightforward as it seemed, as Beatrix explained to Norman in her letter to him of 12 February 1904:

> I was very much perplexed about the dolls' house, I would have gone gladly to draw it, and I should be so *very* sorry if Mrs Warne [Fruing's wife Mary] or you thought me uncivil. I did not think I could manage to go to Surbiton without

staying [to] lunch. I hardly ever go out, and my mother is so exacting. I have not enough spirit to say anything about it. I have felt vexed with myself since, but I did not know what to do. It does wear a person out.

Again, the inference is clear. Fruing and Mary had invited Beatrix to lunch but Mrs Potter had vetoed the arrangement. A further letter from Beatrix to Norman, dated 18 February 1904, implied that the Warnes had extended their luncheon invitation to include Mrs Potter also, but to no avail:

I don't think that my mother would be very likely to want to go to Surbiton, you did not understand what I meant by 'exacting'. People who only see her casually do not know how disagreeable she can be when she takes dislike. I should have been glad enough to go. I did not know what to do.[12]

Nonetheless, Beatrix was determined to persevere with the project in hand. Six days later she wrote to Norman to thank him for sending her a parcel from Hamleys toy shop in London's Regent Street. It contained the following miniature toys: a ham, a cooking stove, some crockery dishes, and a roast duck. All of these she intended to make use of to illustrate *The Tale of Two Bad Mice*.[13]

As Beatrix had been prevented from seeing the real thing, Norman sent her some photographs of his niece Winifred's dolls' house and, on 20 April 1904, she wrote to thank him. She had then to make do with these photographs as the basis for her sketches. Finally, in that year, *The Tale of Two Bad Mice* was published by Warne, and Beatrix dedicated the book to Winifred Warne, 'the little girl who had the dolls' house'. At about this time Beatrix was also writing a book of nursery rhymes entitled *Appley Dapply*. However, circumstances dictated that it would not be published for another twelve years.

Writing from Lingholm, Derwentwater, on 20 October 1904, Beatrix told Norman that she was to return home to Bolton Gardens in eight days' time, and would be relieved to do so:

> our summer 'holiday' is always a weary business & Keswick pulls me down in August; though quite delightful in autumn when there is a bit of frost.[14]

On her arrival home, she told Harold Warne, 'I am glad to hear the books are doing well, they seem to be in all the shops.'[15] On 17 November Beatrix expressed her frustration to Norman that, owing to domestic duties at Bolton Gardens, she was unable to visit him that day:

> There are so many things I wanted to ask about, it is very disappointing. [However] ... there are muddles here with servants which make me rather tied.[16]

In early December Beatrix sent Norman her sketch of 'The Game of Peter Rabbit', a board game which she had invented in which 'the chances are [naturally!] strongly in favour of Peter' as opposed to Mr McGregor, the owner of the vegetable garden and Peter's worst enemy.[17] She sent Norman, on 3 February 1905, the draft text of two more books, *The Tale of Mr Jeremy Fisher* and *The Tale of The Pie and the Patty-Pan*. In order to produce the illustrations for the former she bought back her 'frog' drawings which she had sold to Ernest Nister & Co. eleven years previously. She was aware that Norman disliked frogs but she hoped to persuade him to look favourably upon the book by saying how convinced she was that her depictions of 'water-forget-me-not, lilies etc ...' would make 'pretty pictures'.[18]

From Beatrix's letter to Norman of 27 February 1905, it is clear that she and he were managing to meet, despite the best efforts of her parents to keep them apart. 'Would Thursday afternoon be convenient to you to look over the hedgehog drawings [for her proposed story *The Tale of Mrs. Tiggy-Winkle*] if I arrange to bring them then?' she enquired.[19] On 21 May, in a letter to

F. Warne & Co., her mood was upbeat: 'I am glad that the old books continue to sell, especially my favourite, *The Tailor*.' (She considered *The Tailor of Gloucester* to be not only her favourite story, but also 'far the best'.)[20] However, when she wrote to Norman again on 18 June, she implied that her parents were still making life difficult for her, remarking that 'I will bring the drawings again tomorrow, unless prevented, *still* in doubt . . .'[21]

With Norman, and perhaps for the first time in her life, Beatrix had a kindred spirit of about her own age in whom she could confide and who could also share her joy in creating her 'tales' and seeing them published. And her happiness was complete when, at Bolton Gardens on Monday 25 July 1905, she received a letter from Norman proposing marriage.[22] By coincidence, Beatrix had written to Norman on the very same day concerning *The Tale of Mrs Tiggy-Winkle*. She also took the opportunity to acquaint him with the fact that she and her parents would be spending their holiday in Wales, and to give him her forwarding address: 'Hafod-y-Bryn' (Welsh for 'The summer dwelling place set on the hill'), Llanbedr, a village in Merionethshire on the north-west coast, where she and her parents would be from the following Thursday, 28 July.[23] In the event, the Potters' departure was postponed, presumably because Norman's proposal had caused an upheaval in the Potter household. Nevertheless, Beatrix accepted Norman's offer of marriage. She was aged thirty-nine, and Norman thirty-seven.

Although Beatrix's parents were opposed to the match, a compromise was agreed. There was to be no public announcement of the engagement, which was to be kept a secret from everyone except the couple's close relations. However, Beatrix could wear the ring that Norman had given her. (As for Norman, the only surviving photograph of him to be taken at the time of his engagement to Beatrix revealed that he also wore an engagement ring, the one that Beatrix had given him.)[24]

Beatrix owed her success, not only to her own talent, but also to the fact that she had chosen an occupation in which she could compete with men on equal terms, and one in which several other women writers and illustrators of children's books had blazed a trail already. And, for her, the proverbial 'icing on the cake' was that she had fallen in love with, and become engaged to, a partner in the firm of Frederick Warne & Co., which was not only her own publisher, but Britain's leading publisher of the day of children's books.

One may ask why Norman proposed to Beatrix by letter rather than in person, and why, prior to that, had he not called on Mr Potter to ask that gentleman for his daughter's hand in marriage, as was then the custom? Was it because he was aware of the hostile reception which he would inevitably have received from her parents? Or was there another, more profound reason, one connected with his health?

How did the couple's love affair progress? According to Norman's niece, Winifred (who was only five years old at the time, and must therefore have obtained the information from her family subsequently):

> It was the strangest of courtships. They were never alone together. When Beatrix went to the office [Warne's] she was always chaperoned and when she went to [Norman's home] Bedford Square some other member of the family would always be there, too ...[25]

Soon, another black cloud, this time of a far more serious nature, appeared on the horizon. On 30 July Beatrix, who had not yet left with her parents for Wales as planned, wrote a letter to Harold Warne from 51 Minster Road, West Hampstead, the home of her former governess, Florrie Hammond, with whom she was staying. In it she expressed her anxiety about the health of Norman, who had evidently been on a sales visit to Manchester, but had by then returned:

> I do trust that your brother is not going to be very ill, I got scared before he went to Manchester, wondering if he had been drinking bad water.[26]

Beatrix visited the Warne household on Monday 1 August, bearing a gift for Norman her fiancé, who, as she feared, *had* been taken ill. The gift was a drawing which she had done, some years previously, of the pumpkin carriage which fetched the fairy-tale character, Cinderella, from the ball. The carriage was drawn by three pairs of rabbits, with mice and other animals in attendance. Whether she gave it to Norman in person, or gave it to Harold to give to him, is not known, but the inference is obvious. Beatrix was 'Cinderella', and Norman her newly-found 'Prince'![27] Finally, on or about Thursday 4 August, the Potter family departed for Wales.

Notes

1. Linder, *The Journal of Beatrix Potter from 1881–1897*, June 1894.
2. Lane, Margaret, *The Tale of Beatrix Potter*, p. 76.
3. Beatrix to Norman Warne, 8 May 1902. Taylor, *Beatrix Potter's Letters*, pp. 60 & 62.
4. Beatrix to Norman Warne, 22 May 1902. Taylor, *Beatrix Potter's Letters*, p. 62.
5. Beatrix to Norman Warne, 10 May 1903. Taylor, *Beatrix Potter's Letters*, p. 75.
6. Beatrix to Norman Warne, 20 August 1903. Taylor, *Beatrix Potter's Letters*, p. 80.
7. Beatrix to Norman Warne, ? September 1903. Taylor, *Beatrix Potter's Letters*, p. 81.
8. Beatrix to Norman Warne, 30 January 1905. Taylor, *Beatrix Potter's Letters*, p. 112.
9. 'Johnny Crow' was a fictitious character who features in *Johnny Crow's Garden: A Picture Book*, by artist and writer Leonard Leslie Brooke.
10. Linder, *A History of the Writings of Beatrix Potter*, p. 150.
11. Lane, op. cit., p. 78.
12. Beatrix to Norman Warne, 18 February 1904. Taylor, *Beatrix Potter's Letters*, p. 86.
13. Beatrix to Norman Warne, 24 February 1904. Taylor, *Beatrix Potter's Letters*, p. 88.
14. Beatrix to Norman Warne, 20 October 1904. Taylor, *Beatrix Potter's Letters*, p. 104.
15. Beatrix to Harold Warne, 25 October 1904. Taylor, *Beatrix Potter's Letters*, p. 104.
16. Beatrix to Norman Warne, 17 November 1904. Taylor, *Beatrix Potter's Letters*, p. 108.
17. Beatrix to Norman Warne, 7 December 1904. Taylor, *Beatrix Potter's Letters*, p. 110.

18. Beatrix to Norman Warne, 3 February 1905. Taylor, *Beatrix Potter's Letters*, p. 112.
19. Beatrix to Norman Warne, 27 February 1905. Taylor, *Beatrix Potter's Letters*, p. 114.
20. Beatrix to F. Warne & Co., 21 May 1905. J Taylor, *Beatrix Potter's Letters*, p. 117.
21. Beatrix to Norman Warne, 18 June 1905. Frederick Warne Archives.
22. This date is deduced from a letter which she wrote to Norman's sister, Millie, on 1 February of the following year, in which she refers to 'the 26th, the day after I got Norman's letter'. Beatrix to Millie, 1 February 1906. L. p. 139. The 26th was a Tuesday, and the letter no longer exists.
23. Beatrix to Norman Warne, 25 July 1905. Taylor, *Beatrix Potter's Letters*, p. 123.
24. Lane, *The Magic Years of Beatrix Potter*, p. 136.
25. Comments by Winifred Warne in Taylor, Joyce Irene Whalley, Anne Stevenson Hobbs, and Elizabeth M. Battrick, *Beatrix Potter: The Artist and Her World*, p. 99.
26. Beatrix to Harold Warne, 30 July 1905. Taylor, *Beatrix Potter's Letters*, p. 124.
27. Beatrix to Millie Warne, 15 July 1917, Cotsen Children's Library, Princeton University, New Jersey, USA, in Lear, *Beatrix Potter: A Life in Nature*, p. 200.

CHAPTER 17

Norman's Tragic Death

D URING HER time in Wales, to where the Potters travelled by train, Beatrix kept a holiday diary, and it was the following entry which was, as it transpired, the most significant:

> August 24 [1905]. A still grey day after rain. In the morning I went up [to] the wood & sat on a seat there writing to my aunt. I was reading a letter [presumably either from Norman, or from Norman's sister Millie] that made me think him [Norman] very bad [i.e. ill], but I am slow at taking things in & I was quite quiet ... After lunch I took my bunnies down into the cellar, and perhaps because it was a little dark & damp I got rather depressed & *most mercifully* I wrote to my dear old man [i.e. Norman] – the letter he got the last morning. I soon wrote myself quite merry again, & it is a silly letter all about my rabbits ... – but he didn't read it, so it was good enough. I am so thankful I wrote it.[1]

The dreadful significance of Beatrix's words, 'the last morning', and 'he didn't read it' was about to become clear. She continued:

> I got my sketching things & went down to the village to post my letter, how well one remembers every sound & every

person one met ... I got over some steps on the bridge-wall into a meadow ... I went on through the farm yard & saw some more things worth doing [i.e. worth painting or sketching], it looked so pretty in the slanting light – a very old low cottage with a flat roof & much great slabs of slate. There was a great stone coffin opposite the door under a pump, [used] as a drinking trough for the cattle. I am ashamed if I am superstitious but it made me jump!

After tea I went out again to draw a field of barley shooks [stooks] below the Barmouth Road ... The railway ran just below – A white train of north western [railway] carriages ran past towards the south. I wondered if it was going through to Euston, I wished vaguely I was in it & thought about my [luggage] box that was packed. I am *quite* glad now I was not in time, I should only have cried & upset him, and I am sure he would have sent for me if he had wanted me, for I had told him I would come any time if he found the separation too trying. They [Norman's family] did not send a wire to Llanbedr till next morning, [due] I suppose [to] some regulation about country [post] offices. It was merciful to me anyhow, for I do not think there was another night train after that one I was looking at ...

I remember thinking the evening was as still as death – and as beautiful – as I was looking at it there came out through the mist over the sea just for a few seconds – a gleam of – golden sunshine – 'In the evening there shall be Light.'[2]

Beatrix's premonition proved to be a prophetic one, for the following morning, Friday 25 August 1905, she received a telegram from the Warne family summoning her, as Norman was dying. She and her parents returned to London, but by the time they had done so it was too late. On the afternoon of that same day, only a month to the day after he had proposed to Beatrix, the thirty-seven-year-old Norman died at his home, 8 Bedford Square.

Four days later Norman was buried at London's Highgate Cemetery. Whether or not Beatrix attended the funeral is not known. However, a letter written by her later that year to Norman's sister, her dear friend Millie Warne, indicates that she had viewed Norman's body after his death. In this letter she referred to her aunt, Clara Potter, who also died in 1905. Her deceased aunt's face, she said, was 'tired' and 'rather cross . . . so very different to Norman's'.[3] Norman's death was certified by Arthur Ricketts MD, who recorded that the former had died of 'Lymphatic Leucocythaemia [duration] 2½ months', and that his brother, Fruing Warne, was present at the death.[4] Curiously, there was no mention of Beatrix in Norman's will.

It is not unusual for a person to recall exactly what he or she was doing at about the time of the death of a loved one, particularly if that loved one was very much loved, and if the death was unexpected, and Beatrix was no exception in this respect. Looking back, she could recall everything that she saw and did on the day before Norman died, and her diary entry for 24 August 1905 is one of the most poignant passages in the English language. The memory of that day, and the emotions that she felt, would become etched permanently into her memory. And from that time forward life would never be the same again. An image of the beautiful Lake District on a lovely evening had imprinted itself on her mind. How she must have wished that she could have frozen that moment of her life and had the power to change its future direction. Norman's health would be restored, her parents would acquiesce to their marriage, and she and he could make a home together where they could laugh and be happy in the perfect union of two kindred spirits. Alas, it was not to be.

Norman was now no longer with her. Nonetheless, what did endure was the amicable relationship which she had built up with his family, and also with his publishing company, Frederick Warne & Co.

* * *

Eleven days after her bereavement Beatrix was to be found at Gwaynynog near Denbigh, North Wales, the home of her Uncle

104

Fred Burton. From there she wrote to Harold Warne and from her letter it was apparent that, despite everything, her work for Frederick Warne & Co. was proceeding unabated. Referring to the proof sheets containing the illustrations for *The Tale of Mrs. Tiggy-Winkle*, which had arrived that morning, she declared:

> I like it very much on the whole – if anything I think one or two figures are a trifle too blue – the last one of the hedge-hog running away and the one of the spring might have had more yellow so as to give more grass green effect.

And, referring to her 'Jeremy Fisher' book she said, 'I think I had convinced Norman that I could make it a really pretty book with a good many flowers & water plants for background.' But she revealed to Harold that she was far from happy:

> I am moving from this terrible address on Saturday to lodgings ... I think unless anything went wrong at home, I shall stay away 2 months; but I shall want to come to London in the middle of the time to get the projected new books looked over and to see dear Millie again. I feel as if my work and your kindness will be my greatest comfort. [and she ends the letter] Believe me yrs very sincerely Beatrix Potter.[5]

The phrase 'terrible address' may have reflected the fact that Uncle Fred Burton, of whom Beatrix was very fond, was also in mourning, his wife Harriet (née Leech) having died four months previously.

Reading between the lines, the above paragraph says it all. The Potters had placed every conceivable obstacle in the path of her engagement to Norman, before finally accepting it only reluctantly. And now Norman was dead and, for the time being at least, she found it impossible to contemplate being in their company. She therefore intended to have a two-month break from her parents and when she finally did return to London her primary objective would be to see not them, but Millie, her 'greatest comfort', and also Millie's brothers (with whom she wished to discuss her books).

A remark which Beatrix made to 'one of the Gloucestershire cousins', probably Caroline, that 'publishing books is as clean a trade as spinning cotton',[6] gives an important clue as to why the Potters had been so steadfastly opposed to her attachment to the late Norman Warne. The implication is that Beatrix's parents looked down on Norman because he was 'in trade'. Beatrix, on the other hand, could easily have pointed out that in this he was no different from her own family's (Potter and Leech) forebears who had made their fortunes in the cotton trade.

For their part the Potters could have pointed out to Beatrix, and probably did, just how 'well' other members of the family had done. For example, of Beatrix's maternal cousins, Ethel Leech married the Reverend Sir William Hyde Parker, tenth Baronet, of Melford Hall, Suffolk; John Leech II's son, John Henry Leech (III), became his father's heir, and Stephen Leech rose to a high position in the Diplomatic Service. And Beatrix's paternal cousin Margaret Roscoe married Sir Charles Mallet, formerly MP for Plymouth and Under-Secretary for War in the Liberal Government. It is understandable, therefore, with family pedigrees such as these, that the Potters should not only have hoped, but also expected, that Beatrix would marry well.

In late September 1905 Beatrix returned to London as planned, not to Bolton Gardens, but to 8 Bedford Square, the home of Millie and her mother, Mrs Louisa Warne, and formerly of Norman. From here, on the 26th, she wrote to Mary, wife of Fruing Warne, to thank her for the 'sweet photograph' which she had sent her of her daughters (the late Norman's nieces) Winifred and Eviline. Said she:

> I should have liked it and admired it even if they had been strangers, but I have heard Norman talk so often about the children that they seem like little friends.

She told Mary that she planned to return to North Wales the following day and after that, to visit the Lake District in order to do some sketching:

> I expect I shall go back to London about the end of October, I will write to you as soon as I get back and ask when I may come over to lunch.

She then reiterated to Mary Warne how grateful she was for the kindness shown to her by the family, 'it has been a real comfort & pleasure to stay in this [Mrs Louisa Warne's] house.' Also, she told Mary that she and Millie had visited Norman's grave at Highgate Cemetery the previous day, where she observed that the headstone, which had evidently come loose, had been

> put back quite neatly again; it seems to want something planting at the back ... I was wondering whether white Japanese anemones would grow where it is rather shaded, Millie says you have them in your garden & know their habits.[7]

October 1905 found Beatrix at Sawrey in the Lake District, for reasons which will shortly be discussed. Two days before that Christmas, by which time she had returned to her parents' home at Bolton Gardens, Beatrix told Millie:

> I am sending you a copy of the sketch I did [on] the last evening [i.e. of the day before Norman's death] in the barley field at Llanbedr, I try to think of the golden sheaves, and harvest; he did not live long but he fulfilled a useful happy life. I must try to make a fresh beginning next year. I have had such kind letters and remembrances from your brothers, I do feel rather abashed about their handsome [Christmas] presents when none of mine are done.[8]

And she also told Millie how she had been busy improving the look of her property and straightening 'the old windy road'.

Beatrix was invited to stay with her Aunt Lady Roscoe in February 1906. Lady Roscoe was residing in Bath where her husband, Sir Henry, 'Uncle Harry', was taking the waters. From there she wrote to Millie to say how she was reminded of *Persuasion* which was her favourite of all Jane Austen's novels and which was set in that city. 'I thought my story had [would have] come right with patience & waiting like Anne Eliott's [Elliot] had,' said Jane, in reference to the heroine of the story who had finally, and only after many trials and tribulations, married the hero, Captain Wentworth. Alas, for Beatrix, who herself had waited so long before Norman came into her life, this could never now come to pass and there could be no happy ending.

On 17 August 1906 Beatrix wrote from Lingholm in the Lake District to tell Millie how pleased she was to hear of the birth of Fruing Warne and his wife Mary's third child, Norman Fruing. Then, with her late fiancé Norman in mind, she made Millie a promise:

> I will send you some white heather next week, it would keep in water [for] some time until you could take it to Highgate ...[9] [i.e. to Norman's grave at Highgate Cemetery.]

Early the following month, Beatrix wrote again to Millie, to whom she had now paid a return visit, from Sawrey to say:

> I did so much enjoy staying with you and seeing you all again. Will you write to me at Lingholme next, I shall be going there on Saturday & [am] always glad of a letter when you have time. With much love yrs aff. Beatrix Potter.[10]

Notes

1. Taylor, *Beatrix Potter: A Holiday Diary*, pp. 50–1.
2. Ibid, pp. 52–3. This is a misquotation derived from the *Holy Bible's* Old Testament Book of Zechariah 14:7 '... at evening time it shall be light.'
3. Taylor, op. cit., p. 55.
4. General Register Office: Norman Dalziel Warne. Certified copy of an Entry of Death, Ref. No. DYC 137367.

5. Beatrix to Harold Warne, 5 September 1905. Taylor, *Beatrix Potter's Letters*, p. 126.
6. Lane, *The Tale of Beatrix Potter*, p. 84.
7. Beatrix to Mrs Fruing Warne, 26 September 1905. Taylor, *Beatrix Potter's Letters*, pp. 131–2.
8. Taylor, op. cit., p. 58.
9. Beatrix to Millie Warne, 17 August 1906 Taylor, *Beatrix Potter: A Holiday Diary*, p. 58.
10. Beatrix to Millie Warne, 6 September 1906. Taylor, *Beatrix Potter's Letters*, p. 143.

CHAPTER 18

The Secret of Beatrix's Success

IN CHOOSING to become an author and illustrator of children's books Beatrix would encounter none of the obstacles which had beset her in regard to her scientific paper on the germination of fungal spores for, in this field, no academic qualification or university degree was required, nor was it necessary to belong to an academic society. Instead, this, for women, was a well-trodden path and a sphere of activity in which their talents were recognized and appreciated. And it was a task for which Beatrix was supremely equipped; by the time she had embarked upon the writing of *The Tale of Peter Rabbit* in early 1900, she was a highly competent artist who had already spent almost two decades of her life visiting art galleries in the capital and around the country, examining the paintings therein with a critical eye and making, in her journal, copious critical notes of what she had seen.

When she came to create the illustrations for her book, this experience, together with the painting lessons which she had received over the course of several years, stood her in fine stead. Also, her studies of natural history came in useful when it came to illustrating her 'tales' in which, in addition to the main characters of the stories, there appeared butterflies, a housefly, snails, fish, water lilies, and, of course, fungi.

It is generally acknowledged that everything about Beatrix's illustrations for *The Tale of Peter Rabbit* is delightful: the perfect composition of each painting, the delicate brushwork, the harmony of the colours, and the portrayal of the little creatures going about their daily lives. We are enchanted by the antics of 'Peter' as he nibbles away at a radish, becomes entangled in a gooseberry net, wriggles frantically under the gate of Mr McGregor's garden, and scampers away in order to avoid the rapidly descending garden sieve as the furious McGregor threatens to crush him beneath it. Only someone who had made meticulous observations of the behaviour of such animals and understood them totally could have produced such delightful masterpieces. In fact, to Beatrix, the characters portrayed in her 'tales' were the reincarnations of her pets, which she knew and loved, with a few extra ones added in for good measure. Witness, for example, this extract from her diary, where she described how her real-life rabbit, Peter, entertained the children of Mrs W. Bruce of Hyde Park Square when they came to tea at Bolton Gardens:

> Peter Rabbit was the entertainment, but flatly refused to perform although he had been black-fasting [a Scottish phrase meaning 'refraining'] all day from all but mischief. He caused shrieks of amusement by getting up in the arm-chair and getting on to the tea-table ... He really is good at tricks when hungry, in private, jumping (stick, hands, hoop, back and forward), ringing [a] little bell and drumming on a tambourine.[1]

Neither could Beatrix's illustrations have been executed by someone who did not have a deep and abiding love of the animal kingdom. (No wonder publishers Hildesheimer & Faulkner, and also Ernest Nister, had 'snapped up' some of her previous works of art.)

During the four decades which followed the publication of *The Tale of Peter Rabbit* in 1902, no fewer than thirty-three works by Beatrix were published, including another twenty of her 'tales' (and a further thirteen volumes were published after her death). What was the secret of her success?

Beatrix, as she herself declared, took immense pains when producing her artwork. Where possible, she drew from life, selecting one or other of her pets as a model for the character that would one day appear in whichever 'tale' she happened to be working on at the time. Otherwise, (like Caldecott) she took the trouble to visit local museums, in particular the Natural History Museum at South Kensington, where she examined stuffed specimens and skeletons in order to replicate exactly the features of the creatures that she chose to portray. There was nothing abstract about her work for, as she once told Delmar Banner (the artist who painted her portrait), 'I can't invent, I only copy.'[2]

Beatrix was fortunate in having her brother Bertram to criticize her work where he felt it appropriate. For example, on 2 May 1902, she had written to Norman Warne in respect of drawings that she had created for her Peter Rabbit book (and which Warne had asked her to amend) to say:

> My brother is sarcastic about the figures; what you & he take for Mr McGregor's nose, was intended for his ear not his nose at all.[3]

As she herself admitted she was not adept when it came to the portrayal of the human figure. However, this is where her camera came in useful. Whilst staying at Kalemouth, Roxburghshire, Scotland, for example, she took a photograph of the cook, which she copied and reproduced in *The Tale of Peter Rabbit*. Likewise, at Sawrey, she photographed a neighbouring farmer, John Postlethwaite, who subsequently appeared as 'Farmer Potatoes' in *The Roly-Poly Pudding*.

The majority of children who read Beatrix's 'tales' were town and city dwellers who would not have been familiar with the vast majority of animals which featured in them. However, even

Beatrix, by Birnam photographer A. F. MacKenzie. (*Photo: Chapter House Museum, Dunkeld, Perthshire*)

William Heelis at Hawkshead (In *Tale of Mrs W. Heelis*). (*Photo: John Heelis*)

Helen Beatrix Potter as a child. (*Photo by Rupert Potter: The Beatrix Potter Society*)

Beatrix and her governess at Dalguise. (*Photo by Rupert Potter: The Beatrix Potter Society*)

Beatrix, Mr Potter, Bertram, and Mrs Potter at Dalguise. (*Photo by Rupert Potter: The Beatrix Potter Society*)

The Wide Wide World, by Elizabeth Wetherell

"YOU SEE THAT LITTLE WHITE VILLAGE YONDER?"

Herbert Strang's Library

The WIDE
WIDE
WORLD
◆
ELIZABETH
WETHERELL

HUMPHREY · MILFORD
OXFORD · UNIVERSITY
· PRESS ·
LONDON

Beatrix with 'Spot'. (*Photo by Rupert Potter: The Beatrix Potter Society*)

Charles McIntosh.
(*Photo by James McIntosh*)

John Bright and John
Everett Millais, by
Rupert Potter.
(*Photo: Blair Castle Archives*)

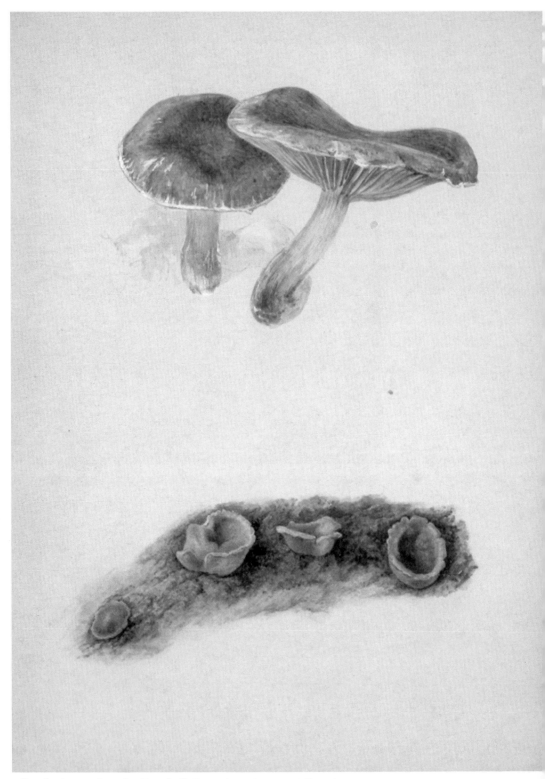

Stropharia aeruginosa by Beatrix Potter. (*Photo: The Armitt Collection*)

Sir Henry E. Roscoe

Beatrix and the Reverend William Gaskell at Dalguise. (*Photo by Rupert Potter: The Beatrix Potter Society*)

'A Dream of Toasted Cheese', presented to Sir Henry Roscoe by his niece Beatrix Potter

Sir William Thiselton-Dyer. (*Photo: The Royal Botanic Gardens, Kew*)

James Martineau

Norman Dalziel Warne.
(*Photo: Frederick Warne*)

George Massee. *(Photo: The Royal Botanic Gardens, Kew)*

Joseph Moscrop in 1919. *(Photo: Rosalind Moscrop;* BP's Farming Friendship. *Cover. Beatrix Potter Society)*

Noel Moore.

Lillie Langtry, 1879,
by Rupert Potter.
(*Photo: Blair Castle
Archives*)

Beatrix in later life.

(*Left*) Amelia Louise Warne ('Millie'). (*Photo: Frederick Warne*)

(*Right*) Pen and ink sketch by Beatrix of two Herdwick sheep and a duck, a present given to Marry F. Gill and the Field family of Massachusetts, USA, on the occasion of Beatrix's 58th birthday, 28 July 1924.

Lady Ulla Hyde Parker

country children, who *were* familiar with such creatures, would, in all probability, never have studied them and their habits in anything like the depth that Beatrix did. For example, in this letter to Winifrede Moore, she said:

> I must tell you a funny thing about the guinea hens here. You know what they are like I daresay; grey speckled birds with very small silly heads. One day, Parton, the coachman, saw them running backwards and forwards in the field, bobbing their heads up & down & calling out Pot rack! pot rack! pot rackety rack! They were watching something white which was waving about in the long grass. Parton could not tell what it was either, till he got close to it, when up jumped a fox! It had been lying on its back waving its tail to make the silly guinea hens come near it.[4]

Beatrix's attention to detail also extended to the apparel which her fictional characters wore, and to the artefacts which appeared in the stories. She visited the South Kensington Museum where, amongst 'some most beautiful eighteenth century clothes', she hoped to discover a coat which she could copy which would be a suitable attire for the *Tailor of Gloucester*.[5] She was, however, aware of her limitations and when Warne asked her if she would take on some extra work she declared that this would require 'more capacity for drawing children & birds, than I possess'.[6]

When searching for a second bookcase to feature in *The Tale of Two Bad Mice*, Beatrix had told Norman Warne that her Uncle Fred Burton 'knew of a real good one in Denbigh, a Sheraton bureau it is such a beauty; Johnny Crow [i.e. Norman himself] would appreciate the joiner's work inside it'.[7]

Beatrix was involved not only with creating her books, but also with their presentation. For example, on 25 April 1902, she wrote to Warne to say:

> I have been wondering whether the rabbit on the cover [of *The Tale of Peter Rabbit*] ought not to face the other

way, towards the binding; it would not take long to copy [it] again.[8]

Sometimes, despite her enthusiasm, she found her work to be an exhausting process, as indicated in a letter she wrote to Warne on 8 May 1902:

> I wish that the drawings had been better ... but I am becoming so tired of them I begin to think that they are positively bad.[9]

Beatrix has been compared with illustrator Randolph Caldecott and she once admitted that he was the only artist whom she had 'really tried to copy ...'.[10] (Later in life, she expressed regret that she had never had the opportunity of meeting Caldecott in person.)[11] Nevertheless, she confessed that she 'did *not* achieve much resemblance [i.e. to Caldecott's work]'.[12]

Despite what Beatrix said there *is* a resemblance between her work and that of Caldecott. The latter's 'Mr Rat', for example, has a similar outline to the former's 'Mr Samuel Whiskers'. Closer inspection, however, reveals that Beatrix uses variation of light and colour far more effectively, and achieves a three-dimensional quality to her painting which is absent in Caldecott's work.

The fact that Beatrix, wherever possible, drew her figures from life meant that each individual hair on the bodies of her furry characters is portrayed, and the sheen on the coats of the Flopsy bunnies and the meticulous detail of Mrs Tiggy-Winkles' whiskers gives an almost tangible impression. Not only that but when her animal characters are engaged in animal-like activities, she, as a keen observer of nature, was able to portray this with deep insight and feeling. Another advantage that Beatrix had over both Caldecott and Crane was that their illustrations were done to order, whereas she was the unconstrained creator, both of the narrative *and* of the illustrations. This meant that the style and freshness of the finished product was on a level which her rivals could not possibly attain.

As already stated, Beatrix was well read, having been exposed to a wide variety of literature as a child and this, of course, had a bearing on her own writing. She was aware that the idea of conflict was at the heart of all good stories, and this is true of her narratives where a cat preys on a mouse, a fox on a duck, and where human beings, such as Mr McGregor, can be a danger to creatures like Peter Rabbit.

The names she chooses for her animal characters are both appealing, for one reason or another, and entirely apposite: 'Mr Tod' implies a degree of menace, 'Mr Samuel Whiskers', one might guess was a rat, even without seeing him, and what more obvious than 'Squirrel Nutkin' or 'Jemima Puddle-Duck', appellations which roll delightfully off the tongue and dwell forever in the memory. However, Beatrix was not overly sentimental about her fictional characters for she knew, from her own experience, that real-life animals, just like humans, could be vicious and bad-tempered. Said she, in a letter to Harold Warne:

> Tell Louie [Harold's daughter, Alice Louisa] I shall have to teach her kitten manners. I was scratched fearfully by the original manx Tom. I had to whip him.[13]

Those who read her 'tales' are beguiled by the fact that her 'characters' are both animal and human at the same time, a feature which makes them so endearing. Squirrel Nutkin gathers nuts to eat, Miss Moppet the kitten catches a mouse and teases it, and the sinister Mr Tod, in anticipation of a nice meal, attempts to lure Jemima Puddle-Duck into his residence. On the other hand, Mrs Tiggy-Winkle the washerwoman uses an iron, Old Brown the owl sits at a table and uses a spoon to eat honey from a plate, Ginger the cat and Pickles the terrier have their own village shop, and Tommy Brock the badger uses a spade for digging. Mischievous behaviour is commonplace, as when Peter Rabbit steals from Mr McGregor's garden, and this is what children love. However, discipline and morality are also themes which feature strongly in the 'tales' as, for example, when Mr Bunny whips his son Benjamin with a switch for misbehaving, and when Tom Thumb, one of the two bad mice, breaks some items in the dolls' house and duly does the decent thing by paying for the damage.

In her storytelling Beatrix was also able to draw upon her knowledge of botany. For example, in *The Tale of Mr. Tod*, Mr Bouncer offers Tommy Brock, the badger, a glass of his daughter Flopsy Bunny's cowslip wine, and in *The Fairy Caravan*, Paddy Pig suffers from hallucinogenic effects after eating toadstool tartlets. And in her short story entitled 'A Walk amongst the Funguses' Beatrix is able to write with the confidence of some-one who had studied the subject of mycology in great detail. 'The Boletus ... sat out in the sun, drying its sticky cap', whereas the Cantharella 'was like a very tall cream-coloured umbrella with brown spots on top, and a white fringe round its waist'.

It was Lady Ulla Hyde Parker who identified what was most appealing about the characters in Beatrix's 'tales'.

> Personality is really the right word, for her animals did become people, real people, by the time she had depicted them in line and colour, making them do and say all sorts of things.[14]

Notes

1. Linder, *The Journal of Beatrix Potter from 1881–1897*, 18 November 1895.
2. Lane, *The Magic Years of Beatrix Potter*, p. 99.
3. Beatrix to Norman Warne, 2 May 1902. Taylor, *Beatrix Potter's Letters*, p. 61.
4. Beatrix to Winifrede Moore, undated letter. National Trust.
5. Beatrix to Norman Warne, 27 March 1903. Taylor, *Beatrix Potter's Letters*, p. 73.
6. Beatrix to F. Warne & Co., 21 February 1904. Taylor, *Beatrix Potter's Letters*, p. 87.
7. Beatrix to Norman Warne, 3 March 1904. Taylor, *Beatrix Potter's Letters*, p. 89.
8. Beatrix to F. Warne & Co., 25 April 1902. Taylor, *Beatrix Potter's Letters*, p. 60.
9. Beatrix to F. Warne, 8 May 1902, Taylor, *Beatrix Potter's Letters*, p. 61.
10. Beatrix to Janet Adam Smith, 2 February 1943. Taylor, *Beatrix Potter's Letters*, p. 454.

11. Beatrix to Jacqueline Overton, 7 April 1942. Morse, *Beatrix Potter's Americans: Selected Letters*, p. 180.
12. Beatrix to Arthur Stephens, 7 February 1943. Taylor, *Beatrix Potter's Letters*, p. 455.
13. Beatrix to Harold Warne, 9 February 1907. Taylor, *Beatrix Potter's Letters*, p. 150.
14. Hyde Parker, *Cousin Beatie: a Memory of Beatrix Potter*, p. 8.

CHAPTER 19

Beatrix and Politics:
Mr W. E. Gladstone

MR AND MRS Potter's forebears were almost universally Liberal in their politics and, from 1861 to 1874, Beatrix's paternal grandfather, Edmund Potter, had been Liberal MP for Carlisle. As for Beatrix, when she grew older she became greatly interested in politics, as her journal indicates, and Mr Potter, a member of London's Reform Club which was a bastion of Liberalism, would have kept her abreast of the burning political issues of the day. She also gleaned information from *The Times* newspaper, of which she was an avid reader. However, it should be remembered that women were not permitted to vote until the passing of the Equal Franchise Act of 1928.

Mr Potter, despite being a member of the Reform Club, was a Conservative (or 'Tory').[1] Beatrix, however, declared that she was a 'Whig', by which she presumably meant a Liberal. (The Whigs were a political party whose fortunes had waned in the late eighteenth century. From the mid-nineteenth century onwards, former Whigs became leading members of the new Liberal Party.) Between 1868 and 1895 the Liberal Party was in and out of office several times, during which period its leader, William Ewart

('W. E.') Gladstone, became Prime Minister on no less than four occasions. However, he was a person for whom Beatrix had neither affection nor respect.

Beatrix's political beliefs tended to be based on deep conviction and they were therefore immutable. For example, she took it for granted that Britain would rule the world, or a huge proportion of it, forever, through the Empire. Also, she was bitterly opposed to the policy, as advocated by the Liberals, of home rule for Ireland, a concept which she considered to be treasonable. And she was understandably alarmed by the activities of the extreme Irish separatists who, supported by Irish-Americans, were engaged in the process of dynamiting, sometimes successfully, government offices, important bridges, railway stations and other buildings in Britain's capital city. In March 1883, referring to an attempt by Irish extremists to blow up government offices in London's Parliament Street, Beatrix declared, 'Papa says it is Mr Gladstone's fault. He takes the side of these rogues ...'[2]

At other times Beatrix adopted a more pragmatic approach. For example, in 1910, she was busy making and printing posters to promote 'tariff reform', whereby the volume of goods imported into Britain from countries outside the British Empire was to be restricted. Her strong feelings on the subject were based on the fact that she had failed to find a British manufacturer to produce copies of a 'Peter Rabbit' doll (which she herself had made and patented), the reason being that the shops were full of cheaper toys made in Germany. At the same time, she campaigned against proposals for a tax on the capital appreciation of land and property (which became law with the passing of the Finance Act, 1909–1910).

> The land tax clauses are almost impossible to understand. I have one expensive field which would be liable to the special ½d. on its capital value, an extra 12/5½ per year. If the tax is raised, I shall be obliged reluctantly to raise the rent (on the field).[3]

Of Gladstone's political opponent, the Conservative politician Lord Randolph Churchill, Beatrix thought more highly, and yet she had reservations even about him. Churchill, she said, was

> looked upon with mingled hope and fear. He is the only promising and spirited young politician who has the spirit to go on his own path, but he wants [i.e. lacks] steadiness. He shows keenness and common sense one day, but the next his followers may find themselves the laughing stock of the country.[4]

Beatrix followed the fortunes of General Charles George Gordon whose forces were fighting a war in the Sudan in support of the Egyptian authorities and against the revolutionary forces of Mohammed Ahmed (The 'Mahdi'). When, on 5 February 1885, news came that the country's capital, Khartoum, had fallen to the rebels and that Gordon was a prisoner, Beatrix described this occurrence as 'awful'. Once again she directed her anger at Gladstone who had procrastinated for five long months before sending Lord Wolseley to relieve the British general, by which time it was too late. Khartoum had fallen and Gordon had been killed two days before Wolseley's relief force arrived. Said Beatrix, angrily, in her journal:

> Oh, if some lunatic had shot old Gladstone 12 months since ... surely, our cowardly Cabinet who are responsible for it would go down? [5]

Beatrix described, on 19 February 1885, how her father was incensed by what he considered to be Gladstone's negligence in this matter, and when he encountered that gentleman in Bond Street he had refused to remove his hat and instead walked straight on. 'I'd have stopped and given him [a piece of] my mind,' declared Beatrix. [6]

Prior to the elections of November 1885 Beatrix stated that, even though she was 'a Whig', nevertheless she hoped that the Conservatives would win, for 'anything is better than the

Radicals'.[7] (The Radicals were a party political faction which advocated change and reform, but whose more extreme elements advocated revolution. However, bearing in mind the gratuitous violence which had occurred during the French Revolution of 1789–99, the Potters, Beatrix included, would have held up their hands in horror at the prospect of such an event occurring in Britain.) In fact, the Liberals won most seats in the election, though not an overall majority, with the result that the Irish Parliamentary Party held the balance of power with the Conservatives. On 13 December 1885 Beatrix noted in her journal that Gladstone, who had now been succeeded as prime minister by the Conservative Marquess of Salisbury, was rumoured to be 'trying to make terms with the Home Rulers at any price'.[8]

After the elections of July 1892 Gladstone formed a minority government which was dependent on the Irish Parliamentary Party for support. The following month Beatrix was moved to declare that Liberal politician Joseph Chamberlain, an opponent of the Home Rule for Ireland Bill, which Gladstone had placed before Parliament in April 1886

> will be the most popular man in the country some day when Mr. Gladstone is gone. [However] the pity of it is he is not completely reliable himself in some ways.[9]

In other words, whoever the politician of the day might be, Beatrix regarded him with a healthy degree of scepticism.

Notes

1. Linder, *The Journal of Beatrix Potter from 1881–1897*, 24 November 1885.
2. Ibid, 16 March 1883.
3. Linder, *A History of the Writings of Beatrix Potter*, p. 403.
4. Linder, *The Journal of Beatrix Potter from 1881–1897*, 2 July 1884.
5. Ibid, 5 February 1885.
6. Ibid, 19 February 1885.
7. Ibid, 23 November 1885.
8. Ibid, 13 December 1885.
9. Ibid, 12 August 1892.

CHAPTER 20

The Allure of the Lake District: A New Love

BEFORE describing how Beatrix came to meet the second love of her life, it is first necessary to explain how she established a foothold in the English Lake District which is where the gentleman in question lived.

Although Beatrix and her parents visited many English and Welsh counties, the majority of their holidays were spent either in Scotland or in the Lake District. In fact, by 1896, the Potter family had spent no fewer than seventeen consecutive summer holidays in the Lake District where it was their custom to arrive with 'their servants, their carriage and pair, and Miss Potter with her pony and phaeton'.[1] Beatrix once declared:

> My brother & I were born in London because my father was a lawyer there, but our descent – our interests and our joy was in the north country.[2]

She waxed lyrical about the Lake District's 'pastoral land-scape backed by mountains. It really strikes me that some [of its] scenery is almost theatrical, or ultra-romantic'.[3] Yet she made it clear that it was not only its scenery, but also its people, who attracted her:

> I am descended from generations of Lancashire yeomen and weavers; obstinate, hard headed, *matter of fact* folk ... As far back as I can go, they were Puritans, Nonjurors, Nonconformists, Dissenters.[4]

Beatrix's maternal great grandfather, Abraham Crompton of Chorley Hall, Lancashire (born in 1757), had blazed the trail to the Lake District by purchasing land and a farm at Tilberthwaite Fell near Coniston. Years later the region was lovingly described by Beatrix thus:

> The coppices in Tilberthwaite and in Yewdale which clothe the lower slopes of Holme Fell are specially beautiful; glorious in autumn colours, and in winter & spring.[5]

And she devoted a whole page of her journal to the 'reminiscences of [her] Grandmother Potter', this being Jessie, née Crompton (born 1801), daughter of Abraham Crompton and his wife Alice (née Hayhurst), who would doubtless have told her of her own childhood holidays spent at Tilberthwaite in the early 1800s.

Summer 1896 found the Potters once again in the Lake District at 'Lakefield', a large country house in the village of Near Sawrey, Lancashire. (Near Sawrey, commonly referred to simply as 'Sawrey', was a village with post office, shop, and public house – the Tower Bank Arms. Half a mile away was its neighbour, Far Sawrey.) The gardens of Lakefield overlooked a lake called Esthwaite Water. 'I have often been laughed at for thinking Esthwaitewater [more commonly written as two words] the most beautiful of the Lakes,' said Beatrix.[6] During their stay, coachman David Becket, who accompanied them, lodged with Farmer Henry Preston at Hill Top Farm, a property which was soon to play a significant role in Beatrix's life. When, on

17 November 1896, their holiday at Sawrey came to an end, Beatrix wrote in her journal:

> I was very sorry to come away in spite of the broken weather. It is as nearly perfect a little place as I ever lived in, and such nice old-fashioned people in the village.[7]

However, the Potters returned to Lakefield for the summers of 1900 and 1902.

When, in the summer of 1905, Hill Top Farm, Sawrey, came on to the market, Beatrix agreed to buy it using royalties from the sale of her books (six of which had been published to date), together with a small legacy from her aunt Harriet Burton, who had died the previous May.[8] Although the death, in late August 1905, of her fiancé, Norman Warne, shattered any dreams that she may have had of him spending holidays with her at Hill Top after their intended marriage, nevertheless, she went ahead with the purchase, which was completed in late summer. At the age of thirty-nine she would have a home of her own for the very first time, albeit a second home, for like all single, Victorian women she was expected to put the needs of her parents first. Mrs Potter, who was always having difficulties with her servants, seemed incapable of managing without Beatrix for any length of time, whereas Mr Potter's problems were of an intermittent, but potentially more serious, nature. For years he had suffered from what Beatrix described as 'gravel'. 'My father is becoming very yellow, and lower than ever,' said she in February 1886 and a decade later, in February 1896, she reported that her father had suffered from an 'Obstruction lasting till Wednesday', the pain from which required him to take 'an extraordinary amount of morphia'.[9] (The conclusion from this is that Mr Potter suffererred from intermittent biliary colic, where sandlike concretions lodge in the biliary tract, causing jaundice, and colic, which is one of the worst pains imaginable.)

All her life Beatrix had dreamt of living in the country and now the chance had come for her to live the dream. And here at Hill Top, she could, for the first time, indulge her homemaking instincts. There would be no question of 'modernizing' this seventeenth-century farmhouse, the character of which would be retained. As for the farm itself, it would continue to be a working entity, run on traditional lines. This would give Beatrix an additional interest, aside from her writings. (She would produce another thirteen books for children over the next eight years.)

To make it possible for farm manager John Cannon and his wife and two children to stay on as her employees, Beatrix arranged for the farmhouse to be extended in a tasteful style which would be in keeping with the original building. Her love of the place is indicated by a delightful pen-and-ink sketch which she made of the farmhouse before the alterations were put in hand. A new dairy was also to be erected. While the building works were in progress she would lodge with Fred Satterthwaite, Sawrey's village blacksmith, and his wife at their cottage, 'Belle Green'.

From a letter that she wrote in October 1905 to Harold Warne, it is clear that Beatrix was in her element. Said she, 'It is most lovely autumn weather, I shall try to stop till end of month if I am not sent for [by her parents].'[10] Four days later, when she wrote to Millie, it was from 'Hill Top Farm, Sawrey, Ambleside.'

Beatrix transferred some of her furniture to Hill Top from London including her 'looking glass' (dressing table mirror) which had once belonged to her great-grandmother, Alice Crompton. Her pair of bellows had been a gift from Norman Warne and she also possessed his umbrella and tobacco pipe, an indication that, although he was no longer with her in person, he remained with her in spirit.[11] Other items of furniture she purchased locally, as when, for example, the contents of a farm were sold at auction (oak being her favourite wood).

Hill Top's interior reflected Beatrix's love of china, particularly Staffordshire, Royal Worcester, Wedgwood, Japanese and Chinese porcelain. On the walls she hung various paintings including *Swiss Cattle* by Randolph Caldecott (1846–86) and the two aforementioned 'frog' prints by Caldecott which her father had purchased for her.

Prior to her arrival at Hill Top Farm there was only a small, walled, kitchen garden in existence. Now she would add a paddock, an orchard, and a flower garden, in the creation of which her knowledge of flowers and plants would be invaluable. A painting by her of her garden would subsequently feature in *The Tale of Tom Kitten* (published in 1907) for which she borrowed a kitten called 'Tom' to use as a model to illustrate the story. Furthermore, Hill Top Farm and the village of Sawrey would provide the setting for further books including *The Tale of Jemima Puddle-Duck* (1908), *The Roly-Poly Pudding* – subsequently called *The Tale of Samuel Whiskers* (1908) and *The Tale of Pigling Bland* (1913).

At Hill Top Beatrix 'kept a few rabbits in a run on the grass in the garden'. This was for the pleasure of any children who came to visit, and who would naturally associate her home with that most famous rabbit of all, 'Peter'![12] And the following paragraph from *The Westmorland Gazette* also reflects her concern for the younger generation:

> The beautiful land she possessed was always available for youth camps, parties, and picnics, and her personal attendance until recently was always assured. Within the last year or so local [Girl] Guides were her guests and [they] welcomed her in costumes depicting characters in her famous little booklets.[13]

Hill Top was Beatrix's escape. There she was far away from unhealthy London, from Bolton Gardens – her 'unloved' home – and its domestic problems, far away from her irritable father (who, admittedly, cannot be blamed for his colic) and from her demanding and inflexible mother, and far away from the Linnean Society and her unfinished business there. Here, a new beginning beckoned. The Lake District, 'Lakeland', is where she found peace. Her cathedrals were the great hills that surrounded her, Coniston, the Langdale Pikes etc. Her paradise was the lush, green landscape beneath. Her hymns were the chants of song-birds and her psalms the musical babbling of brooks.

Another joy for Beatrix was to know that her cousin Edith, the daughter of Mr Potter's younger brother, Walter and his wife Elizabeth, and Edith's businessman husband, Walter Gaddum, lived nearby. They had relocated from Manchester and now resided at a house called 'Brockhole' situated between Windermere and Ambleside. The couple had two children, Walter Frederick and Marjery, to whom, in the late 1890s, Beatrix had sent some of her famous picture letters.

In April 1906 Beatrix was eagerly anticipating a visit from her dear friend Millie Warne, to whom she wrote to say:

> I shall tell Mrs S. [Satterthwaite] to reserve the lodgings. It will be delightful to have you up here at the beginning of May; it is like summer today & the air is so pleasant.[14]

By the end of 1906, when the new wing at Hill Top had been completed, the room above the new farmhouse kitchen became Beatrix's study and library.

During 1907 Beatrix became the proud possessor of two pigs, which she called 'Aunt Susan' and 'Dorcas', six cows, some calves, sheep, hens, ducks, turkeys and chickens.[15] Being a traditionalist, she did not allow 'modern machinery' to be used on her farm. Instead 'She had a lot of hand implements, horses and carts, and a double-horse mowing machine.'[16] Neither did she have a telephone, preferring to use 'the public one at the post office to check up on how her mother was getting on'.[17] And when she was not busy with her farming her favourite indoor pursuits were embroidery and wool spinning.

* * *

In May 1909 Beatrix, who continued to prosper from the sale of her books, purchased another property, Castle Cottage and Farm, the fields of which were immediately adjacent to those of Hill Top Farm. In this, it was solicitors W. H. Heelis & Son of Hawkshead who acted for her, and it was William Heelis, a partner in the firm, who drew up the contract of sale. Three years later, in the winter of 1912/13, William made Beatrix, now aged forty-six, a proposal of marriage. She accepted.

Notes

1. Linder, *A History of the Writings of Beatrix Potter*, p. 168.
2. Biographical profile of Beatrix Potter (Heelis), provided to the editors of *The Horn Book* in November 1942. Quoted in Lear, *Beatrix Potter: A Life in Nature*, p. 9.
3. Linder, *The Journal of Beatrix Potter from 1881–1897*, 29 September 1892.
4. 'Roots of the Peter Rabbit Tales', by Beatrix Potter, *The Horn Book*. May 1929, in Morse, *Beatrix Potter's Americans: Selected Letters*, p. 207.
5. Beatrix to D. M. Matheson, 17 October 1939. Taylor, *Beatrix Potter's Letters*, p. 409.
6. Linder, *The Journal of Beatrix Potter from 1881–1897*, 29 September 1892.
7. Ibid, p. 422
8. 'Roots' of The Peter Rabbit Tales, essay by Beatrix Potter. Published in *The Horn Book* of May 1929. In Morse, *Beatrix Potter's Americans: Selected Letters*, p. 209.
9. Linder, *The Journal of Beatrix Potter from 1881–1897*, 2 February 1896.
10. Beatrix to Harold Warne, 10 October 1905. Taylor, *Beatrix Potter's Letters*, p. 133.
11. Lane, *The Magic Years of Beatrix Potter*, p. 95.
12. Battrick, *The Real World of Beatrix Potter*, p. 52.
13. *The Westmorland Gazette*, 25 December 1943.
14. Beatrix to Millie Warne, 5 April 1906. Taylor, *Beatrix Potter's Letters*, p. 141.
15. Beatrix to Louise Warne, 8 July 1907. Taylor, *Beatrix Potter's Letters*, p. 152.
16. Heelis, *The Tale of Mrs William Heelis: Beatrix Potter*, p. 86.
17. Ibid, p. 87.

CHAPTER 21

William Heelis

ILLIAM, son of the Reverend John Heelis (Rector of Kirkby Thore) and his wife Esther (née Martin), was five years younger than Beatrix, having been born on 2 December 1871. He had five surviving brothers, two of whom were clergymen, and two, like himself, solicitors, and four sisters. A keen athlete and sportsman, William enjoyed shooting, angling, golf, tennis, cricket, and swimming, as well as folk dancing, morris dancing, and billiards.[1] During Beatrix's prolonged periods of absence at her parents' home in London, it was he who had kept her in touch with events at Sawrey. And when he visited her at Hill Top Farm, he arrived on his 'Bradbury' motorcycle, complete with side-car. The first time Lady Ulla Hyde Parker met William, she was most impressed:

> What a kindly face! With a fresh complexion, grey hair and a warm smile he seemed so relaxed and straightforward. He obviously was an uncomplicated person with a practical approach to life.[2]

Ulla also described how William and Beatrix 'could talk for hours about land, farming and sheep'.[3]

When Beatrix wrote to Millie Warne to tell her, in confidence, that she and William Heelis were engaged, she was afraid that, in the circumstances, her dear friend and sister of the late Norman would react unfavourably.

> I have felt very uncomfortable and guilty when with you for some time – especially when you asked about Sawrey. You would be only human if you felt a little hurt! Norman was a saint, if ever man was good. I do not believe he would object ... I certainly am not doing it for thoughtless, light-heartedness.[4]

Millie, however, could not have been more considerate and understanding.

Meanwhile, in 1910, Beatrix's cousin Caroline Hutton had married Francis William Clark, Laird of the Scottish Hebridean Islands of Ulva, Gometra and Little Colonsay. Ever forthright, she now gave Beatrix a piece of advice.

> I advised her to marry him quietly, in spite of them [i.e. Beatrix's parents]. They thought a country solicitor much beneath them ... and she [Beatrix] had the (now) old-fashioned ideas of duty from children to parents, and to excuse them [Beatrix] wrote, 'I see their objections, as we belong to the Bar and the Bench'.[5]

The Lake District was a beautiful place when the weather was clement, but in wintertime conditions could be rigorous indeed. For example, in February 1912, in a letter to Harold Warne, Beatrix declared that 'Conditions are Alpine – 24 degrees of frost last night.'[6] So was Beatrix wise to move from the south of England to the harsher climate of the north, and to involve herself in the manual work that farming required, and especially given the fact that the attack of rheumatic fever which she had sustained as a young woman had weakened her heart? To her, such a question would have seemed irrelevant. Her destiny, as she saw it, was to return to the land of her forebears, there to live the life of her choice, and with her tremendous singlemindedness and willpower, nothing whatever would have deterred her.

In July 1913 Beatrix went on holiday as usual with her parents, this time to 'Lindeth Howe', a Victorian property situated near Bowness-on-Windermere, on the east side of the lake. Here they remained for a period of two months.[7] In late September, by which time they had returned to London, Beatrix was delighted to be able to tell Gertrude, daughter of Dr Henry Woodward, Keeper of Geology at the British Museum, who had once advised her on the eozoon fossil,[8] that:

> William has actually been invited up [presumably to Bolton Gardens] for a weekend soon – they [her parents] never say much, but they cannot dislike him.[9]

On 9 October 1913 Beatrix wrote to Fanny Cooper from 2 Bolton Gardens to say:

> Since coming back here, on Sept 24th with the parents – I have been in bed again either with slight influenza or a very nasty cold. That decides the matter – I am going to get married! I can't keep well in London, and my father is under no obligation to live in town. If he were a poor man or tied to business it would be different. I have felt rather bad – waiting till he was 80 and my mother getting old; but most people are less severe upon me than my own conscience. I rather hope in the end my parents will take a house on lease at Windermere; then it would be all right, for they like him [William Heelis] now they have got over the shock, & he is very nice with old people & anxious to be friendly & helpful. His name is William Heelis, a solicitor living in Hawkshead near Ambleside. They [the Heelises] are a good professional family but not well off – clergymen, lawyers – some have been doctors & bankers ... He is 42 (I am 47) very quiet – dreadfully shy. I'm sure he will be more comfortable married – I have known him six years; he is in every way satisfactory; well known in the district and respected – and he can follow his profession just as conveniently from Sawrey & is fond of the place. My father didn't much

approve the match at first, but I tell him if I had chosen a wealthy man with a place of his own – I should have to have to give up my farm which I am so fond of.

And Beatrix went on to say:

I feel I am deserting my post. But I am of nothing use compared with the nurse – I have more been in the way of doing little things for him [her father], and he won't pay the slightest attention to me – we *both* lose our tempers. When I got engaged last June I was quite of the mind to wait ... but there was a good deal of bother – they were very silly [and] they wouldn't let Mr Heelis come to the house for ever so long – and I think the opposition only made us more fond of one another – he has waited six years already!

I don't think we shall wait much longer – especially if I am going to have bronchial colds in London. I think we shall get married very quietly & go away for a holiday, & then I shall come back home & make a desperate effort to see them settled with some proper attendant.[10]

Beatrix and William were married on 15 October 1913 at the Church of St Mary Abbots, Kensington, in the parish in which Bolton Gardens was situated. An Anglican church was chosen, rather than a Unitarian one, probably as a mark of respect to William and his family who were Anglican, and in particular to William's late father who had been an Anglican minister.

Whatever their misgivings might have been about the match, Mr and Mrs Potter attended the wedding and signed the register. The two other witnesses, a minimum of two for each party being required by law, were William's cousin Lelio Stampa, a lecturer in Modern History at Exeter College, Oxford[11] and Beatrix's friend Gertrude Woodward. The ceremony was conducted by the Reverend Charles S. Durrant, Assistant Curate. Who else was present is not known. (William's father, John, had died in 1893 and his mother, Esther, soon afterwards in the same year.)

It was typical of Beatrix's down-to-earth attitude to life that when she and William returned from their wedding 'there was a white bull-calf in the back of the car', which they had collected, and which was intended for their farm.[12] A week later Beatrix told Millie Warne, 'I am very *happy*, and in every way satisfied with Willie. It is best now not to look back.'[13]

Beatrix decided that she and William would live at Castle Cottage. As for Hill Top, 'I must leave everything here as it is,' she subsequently told Ulla, 'So after I married I just locked the door and left.'[14] Nonetheless, she said, Hill Top remained 'something very precious' to her.[15]

Because certain alterations had to be made to Castle Cottage, it was not until early 1915 that Beatrix and William were able to take up residence there. In the meantime they stayed in a furnished bungalow nearby. And when they did eventually move into Castle Cottage, according to Mrs Mary Rogerson the housekeeper, a sow called 'Sally' 'which became quite affectionate', often shared the dining room with the couple.[16] Meanwhile, the Cannon family continued to reside in their own quarters at Hill Top and manage the farm as before.

In regard to her new life with William, Beatrix quoted the following lines from Act IV, Scene I of William Shakespeare's play, *The Tempest*:

> *Spring came to you at the farthest,*
> *In the latter end of harvest!*[17]

Whether Beatrix's relationship with William reached the same level of emotional intensity as it had with Norman is not known. However, of her fondness for her husband, there can be no doubt. Said she, laughingly, 'When I want to put William in a book [i.e. as a character] – it will have to be as some very tall thin animal.'[18] Needless to say, William was tall and slim! And on another occasion, 'Mr Heelis walks through the toes of his stockings so it is lucky I like darning!'[19] Ulla described Beatrix and William as 'certainly a happy or, perhaps better, contented couple [who] lived harmoniously alongside each other.'[20]

Nonetheless, the elastic thread which stretched between Lakeland and London was soon jerked taut again, when, only thirteen days after her wedding, Beatrix announced that she had been summoned back to London 'as my mother is changing servants'.[21] Despite their daughter's altered circumstances, the Potters were still determined to keep Beatrix at their beck and call, and she, ever the dutiful daughter, was equally determined not to let them down, whatever inconvenience she might suffer as a result.

With her marriage to William Beatrix became absorbed in the life of her home, her now extended farm, and her garden. She also found time for writing and illustrating, and a further nine of her books were published during her lifetime, including *Cecily Parsley's Nursery Rhymes* and *Jemima Puddle-Duck's Painting Book*. In December 1913 she celebrated her first Christmas as Mrs William Heelis.

> It seems strange, to be away [from Bolton Gardens] at this time of year; but I hope my parents do not mind *much* – I mean not specially on account of the time, as we have never kept up anything different for Christmas to a usual Sunday.[22]

To Beatrix's dismay the Christmases which she had experienced at Bolton Gardens had been austere, Unitarian-style affairs, made all the more poignant by what was taking place all around her. A person as well read as she would undoubtedly have heard of Charles Dickens's ghost story *A Christmas Carol* (published in December 1843), and she surely dreamed of engaging in such traditional pursuits as hanging up the Christmas stocking, roasting chestnuts in the fire, and enjoying that special fare which was provided for the Christmas Day feast. She might also have seen the print which appeared in the *Illustrated London News* in 1848 of Queen Victoria, Prince Albert and their children gathered round a Christmas tree. Alas, for her, it was not to be. 'How pretty Miss Paget's tree used to be with the little doll angel at the top,' she wrote wistfully in her journal in reference to her neighbour's daughter, Nina.[23] By contrast, however, for the Potters, the occasion of Queen Victoria's Diamond Jubilee *was* a time for celebration, and, in June 1887, Beatrix and her family 'were very busy arranging our fairy lights, on each of the nine front window sills, seven red in each length, five white above and three blue at the top'.[24] But as the wife of William Heelis, Beatrix had now embarked on a new life, because for the Heelises, Christmas was an occasion to be celebrated.

It was the tradition at Christmastime for members of the extensive Heelis family to assemble at Battlebarrow House, Appleby, home of the Reverend Edward Heelis, William's brother and his wife, Ann, for a 'great family party'.[25] To this, of course, Beatrix was invited. Another festive event which she looked forward to at this time of year was when members of the Sawrey folk-dance group gathered round her pianoforte and sang for her.[26] This was to say 'thank you' to Beatrix for the fact that she

> paid for the materials for the ladies' dresses, and the group really stood out at festivals, with the men in white flannel trousers and white shirts, and the ladies in their dresses of a lovely pink material patterned with roses.[27]

Despite the celebrations William's great-nephew, John Heelis, in his biography of Beatrix stated that neither she nor William were

> particularly religious ... [However, she] rather lent towards the Quakers and was known to have attended the Meeting House at Colthouse near Hawkshead. She certainly had no truck with the local Church of England parson, who said that animals had no souls![28]

But, although Beatrix 'attended no church ... she would talk about the beautiful language of the Bible', said Ulla.[29]

In early 1914 the Potters' need for Beatrix became more acute and she was obliged to make no fewer than eight journeys to London from Sawrey in order to attend to her father who had become seriously ill. Mr Potter finally died on the evening of 8 May 1914, aged eighty-one, the cause of death being cancer of the stomach. He was buried at Hyde Chapel, Gee Cross, Hyde, Cheshire. It was decided that Mrs Potter, now aged seventy-five, should move to the North of England and, to this end, Beatrix found her a furnished property in the village of Sawrey where she was installed with a companion. Beatrix was subsequently relieved to be able to say that her mother was 'comfortably settled here & has been wonderfully contented through some truly awful weather'.[30] Meanwhile, on 4 August 1914, Britain declared war on Germany. In September 1915 Mrs Potter purchased 'Lindeth Howe', Windermere, which her parents had leased in the summer of 1913, which would henceforth be her home.

In 1916 a Miss Eleanor L. Choyce, 'Louie', answered an advertisement by Beatrix for someone to help with odd jobs and gardening. Beatrix developed an abiding affection for Louie who shared her love of singing and dancing. By now the war had taken, and would continue to take, an immense toll in terms of lives lost, a practical effect of this being that the countryside was depleted of manpower. In March 1917 Beatrix was vexed that her ploughman 'has got his calling up [papers, for service in the armed forces] in the very middle of ploughing'.[31]

Sadly, Beatrix's eyesight was deteriorating and when, in May 1918, she sent six drawings to Fruing Warne it was 'in desperation – I simply *cannot* see to put colour in them'.[32] This was for *The Tale of Johnny Town-Mouse*, published in that same year. In that year also, William received his call up papers, but failed the medical examination on account of a knee injury which he had previously sustained whilst playing football. He was therefore exempted from military service.

Whilst there is every indication that Beatrix's marriage to William was a happy one, her late fiancé, Norman, was often in her thoughts and her enduring affection for him is indicated by the fact that, in November 1918, thirteen years after his death and five years after her marriage to William, she was still wearing the engagement ring which he had given her. And, furthermore, she was greatly distressed when she lost it,

> in the corn field – pulled off while lifting wet sheaves with my fingers ... My hand felt very strange & uncomfortable without it.

Fortunately, however, she quickly found it again.[33]

In 1922 Beatrix agreed that William's brother, the Reverend Arthur John Heelis, retired Rector of Brougham near Penrith, who was a bachelor, could come to live with her and William at Castle Cottage. On 14 December 1925 she told Fanny Cooper:

> We have a brother of my husband's who has lived with us for the last three years & he has become more & more of an invalid. He is not a pleasant or a grateful invalid, but we cannot get rid of him, poor man. Such is life! We have to take the rough with the smooth. [34]

The Reverend Heelis died in January 1926.

Notes

1. Heelis, *The Tale of Mrs William Heelis: Beatrix Potter*, p. 23.
2. Hyde Parker, *Cousin Beatie: a Memory of Beatrix Potter*, p. 10.
3. Lane, *The Tale of Beatrix Potter*, p. 110.
4. Ibid, p. 110.
5. Beatrix to Fanny Cooper, 5 January 1911. National Trust.
6. Beatrix to Harold Warne, 3 February 1912. Taylor, *Beatrix Potter's Letters*, p. 196.
7. Beatrix to E. Wilfred Evans, 10 July 1913. Taylor, *Beatrix Potter's Letters*, p. 208.
8. Linder, *The Journal of Beatrix Potter from 1881–1897*, 28 January 1897.
9. Beatrix to Gertrude Woodward, 24 September 1913. Heelis, *The Tale of Mrs William Heelis: Beatrix Potter*, p. 2.
10. Beatrix to Fanny Cooper, 9 October 1913. National Trust.
11. Heelis, *The Tale of Mrs William Heelis: Beatrix Potter*, p. 1.
12. Ibid, p. 5.
13. Lane, op. cit., p. 111.
14. Hyde Parker, op. cit., pp. 21 & 23.

15. Ibid, p. 21.
16. Heelis, op. cit., p. 9
17. Lane, op. cit., p. 157. 'Roots' of The Peter Rabbit Tales, Essay by Beatrix Potter. Published in *The Horn Book* of May 1929. This is a misquotation – the correct one being 'Spring come to you at the farthest. In the very end of harvest!'
18. Beatrix to Margaret Hough, 4 November 1913. Taylor, *Beatrix Potter's Letters*, p. 214.
19. Beatrix to Barbara Buxton, 31 December 1913. Taylor, *Beatrix Potter's Letters*, p. 215.
20. Hyde Parker, op. cit., p. 23.
21. Beatrix to Mrs Martin, 28 October 1913. Taylor, *Beatrix Potter's Letters*, p. 213.
22. Beatrix to Millie Warne, 23 December 1913. Quoted in Lear, *Beatrix Potter: A Life in Nature*, p. 264.
23. Beatrix to Ivy Steel, 30 December 1929, in Maloney, 1977. *Dear Ivy, Dear June: Letters from Beatrix Potter.*
25. Heelis, op. cit., p. 29.
26. Lane, op. cit., p. 160.
27. Taylor, *Through the Pages of Life and My Encounters with Beatrix Potter*, p. 19.
28. Heelis, *The Tale of Mrs William Heelis; Beatrix Potter*, p. 140.
29. Hyde Parker, op. cit., p. 15.
30. Beatrix to Harold Warne, 16 December 1914. Taylor, *Beatrix Potter's Letters*, p. 220.
31. Beatrix to Harold Warne, 19 March 1917. Taylor, *Beatrix Potter's Letters*, p. 232.
32. Beatrix to Fruing Warne, 4 May 1918. Taylor, *Beatrix Potter's Letters*, p. 247.
33. Taylor, *Beatrix Potter: A Holiday Diary*, p. 61.
34. Beatrix to Fanny Cooper, 14 December 1925. National Trust.

CHAPTER 22

Mrs Potter's Latter Years

D ESPITE the passing of the years, the relationship between Beatrix and her mother did not improve. In January 1899, for example, there was another argument over who should have use of the carriage. Beatrix, now aged thirty-two, wished to use it to drive to Wandsworth to visit Annie Moore's eldest daughter, Marjorie, whom she had not seen since the previous July, a fact which she described as 'quite shocking'. However, said she, 'my Mamma wants it to drive the other way'.[1]

Mrs Potter continued to be protective, some would say over-protective, towards her daughter. For example, in August 1905, when the Potters were on holiday in Wales, Beatrix, then aged thirty-nine, wrote in her journal, 'Went to the sea again after lunch, stuffy but rather cold & I was not tempted to paddle in defiance of my Mamma.' Mrs Potter had evidently told Beatrix, now aged thirty-six, that had she paddled, then this would have made her nose bleed![2] There is, however, no obvious association between paddling and a bleeding nose!

Having moved to Lakeland in 1915, Mrs Potter made no concessions to country living when she journeyed 'in her brougham' from her house, Lindeth Howe, across Lake Windermere by ferry to visit her daughter at Castle Cottage every Wednesday afternoon, as was her habit. According to Henry Byers ('Harry'), Beatrix's gardener at Hill Top Farm:

> Mr Beckett the coachman with top hat and cockade would be driving the two horses and Mr Stevens the groom hanging on the back. She [Mrs Potter] always wore black and I never saw her smile. She would stay exactly one hour and then she went back to Lindeth Howe.[3]

And when Beatrix crossed the lake in the opposite direction, in order to repay the visit, the clash of personalities was obvious for, according to Louisa Rhodes (née Towers), Mrs Potter's cook, whom she called 'Lucissa', when Beatrix telephoned her mother at Lindeth How, Mrs Potter would say,

> 'What does she want?' She had abrupt manners, Mrs Potter, in her way – and I heard her say [to Beatrix], 'But you can't have the car to meet you, it's Lucissa's day for shopping.' Mrs Heelis would walk all the way from Sawrey down to the ferry and she was wanting the car to meet her at this side [i.e. Mrs Potter's side of the lake], but Mrs Potter wouldn't let the car go for her before it had taken me shopping for my penny apple. Beatrix used to be raging. She had to walk up this side too. [This was a reference to the long, uphill walk from the lake to Mrs Potter's residence.] They were both very strong willed, you know ...[4]

A period of nine years elapsed between Mrs Potter leaving London in autumn 1915 and the sale of No. 2 Bolton Gardens, and it fell to Beatrix to organize the house clearance:

> I had no sentimental repinnings [repinings] as I had been discontented and never strong as a young person in London – but what a task! and what to keep and what to sell? with a rather imperious old mother awaiting 3 van loads [of her household effects] in Windermere.[5]

Beatrix's letter to Fanny Cooper of 27 December 1924 also indicated that she had no regrets, for of No. 2 Bolton Gardens, she declared that it was 'such a relief to get the house done away with and sold. I was never very well or happy there in old times, and I had no affection for the place'.[6]

In December 1929 Beatrix was aggrieved that her mother had 'steadily taken no interest whatsoever' of her efforts to purchase and preserve as much land as she could of the Lake District.[7] (This will be discussed shortly). And a year later she declared:

> It is annoying that she is so difficult about money – a regular miser in [her] reluctance to spend money, which will simply be wasted in death duties when she has hoarded it up.[8]

And, said Beatrix, when she pointed out 'the unwisdom of saving ... [her mother, Mrs Potter] startled me by making a large unnecessary gift to a relative-in-law'![9] However, as always, there are two sides to the story and it is clear that Mrs Potter was equally annoyed, probably by what she regarded as Beatrix's impertinence.

Beatrix told Fanny Cooper on 15 December 1930 about a visit she had recently made to London:

> I loathe going away from home! Oh the *noise!* And the *crossings* [of the road]! I went out by myself ... and was so afraid of the traffic that I kept a taxi. The cost was an unpleasant surprise; but preferable to being run over ... I don't care if I never see London again.[10]

Lady Ulla Hyde Parker and her husband, Sir William, used to visit Beatrix each summer from 1933 onwards. Ulla became Beatrix's confidante and she describes how Beatrix once told her, after the two of them had paid a visit to Mrs Potter, 'My mother does not approve of me living in a simple farm house. This she doesn't like at all.' Beatrix, it seemed, could never escape her mother's opprobrium.

However, when Mrs Potter died on 20 December 1932, Beatrix, despite their differences, had only pleasant words to say about her late mother. For example, to the Reverend Rawnsley's widow, Eleanor (Rawnsley's second wife whom he had married in 1918, his first, Edith, having died the previous year), she wrote, 'Her chief interests were her canaries, her needlework and her little dog. She was wonderfully clear in mind, but … I am glad that she is at rest.'[11] Mrs Potter was buried, as her late husband had been before her, at Hyde Chapel, Gee Cross, Hyde, Cheshire. *The Westmorland Gazette* reported:

> The passing of Mrs Helen Potter of Lindeth Howe, Storrs, Bowness on Tuesday, caused profound sorrow to a large circle of friends and neighbours, by whom she was held in great affection on account of her courtesy and kindness. Until recently she was able to make occasional visits in her car to the neighbouring village, but her faculties gradually weakened, and her death at the age of 93 years is generally regretted.

Notes

1. Beatrix to Marjorie Moore, 13 January 1899. Victoria & Albert Museum: The Warne Archive.
2. Taylor, *Beatrix Potter: A Holiday Diary*, p. 46.
3. Battrick, *The Real World of Beatrix Potter*, pp. 33–4.
4. Taylor, Joyce Irene Whalley, Anne Stevenson Hobbs, and Elizabeth M. Battrick, *Beatrix Potter: The Artist and Her World*, p. 166.
5. Beatrix to Marian Frazer Harris Perry, 13 July 1936. Morse, *Beatrix Potter's Americans: Selected Letters*, pp. 73–4.
6. Beatrix to Fanny Cooper, 27 December 1924. National Trust.
7. Beatrix to S. H. Hamer, 12 December 1929. Taylor, *Beatrix Potter's Letters*, p. 326.
8. Beatrix to Caroline Clark, 13 December 1930. Taylor, *Beatrix Potter's Letters*, p. 336.
9. Beatrix to S. H. Hamer, 12 December 1929. Taylor, *Beatrix Potter's Letters*, p. 326.
10. Beatrix to Fanny Cooper, 15 December 1930. National Trust.
11. Quoted by Lane, *The Tale of Beatrix Potter*, p. 145.

CHAPTER 23

The Fortunes and Misfortunes of Bertram

EATRIX'S relationship with her brother Bertram was founded on mutual affection and shared interests. However, on her part it was tinged with anxiety, for reasons which will shortly become apparent. In the autumn of 1890 Bertram began a four-year degree course in Classics (Literae Humaniores) at Magdalen College, Oxford. He continued to spend his summer holidays with his family as usual and, when in Scotland or in the Lake District, Beatrix often accompanied him to the river to watch him fish, or into the countryside where he painted, whilst she went in search of fungi. (In one of his sketches he portrays the head and shoulders of his sister Beatrix.) Etching was another of his accomplishments. Like Beatrix, he loved his pets and when he returned to Oxford in the autumn of 1892 for the start of the Michaelmas Term, she recorded that he took with him his pet jay which was 'crammed into a little box kicking and swearing'.[1] Two years later he came down from Oxford, having been awarded a BA; this was a pass degree, and not the more highly-ranked honours degree.

Beatrix took a lively interest in her brother's exploits. Said she of the 1895 festive season, 'We had not a pleasant Christmas, wet,

143

dark, Bertram sulky.'[2] In June 1897 she wrote from Lingholm to Winifrede Moore to say 'My brother has got a jackdaw, a very sly bird. Directly we let him loose he gets into the fireplace and brings out rubbish which has been thrown in the fender.'[3] In October 1902 Beatrix told Winifrede that Bertram had been out ferreting with the gardener and had shot eleven rabbits and some pheasants.[4]

As Beatrix continued to produce the illustrations for her 'tales' so Bertram, when available, made constructive comments and even made alterations to her work when the need arose. For example, in May 1903, she declared 'I am going to meet my brother at the Lakes tomorrow; I think *he* could very likely improve that owl ...'[5] In July 1905 Beatrix complained to Norman Warne that she was 'rather staggered with ... [the] spottyness [sic]' which was apparent on the printing blocks for *The Tale of Mrs Tiggy-Winkle*. 'I have seen my brother's copperplate etchings go exactly the same way, especially if using a mixture of hydrochloric & nitric acid,' she said.[6]

On 30 May 1906 Bertram, after a six-year wait, was elected to his father's club, the Athenaeum. Now aged thirty-four, his occupation was recorded as 'Painter and Etcher'. His proposer was Sir Henry Roscoe and his seconder was shipowner, statistician and social reformer Charles Booth, his original proposer, jute baron and mathematician Sir James Caird, and his original seconder, Sir John Millais, having died in the meantime. Other sponsors included his father, four barristers, an MP, the Canon of St Paul's Cathedral, the King's librarian, the Editor of the *Spectator* and Charles Lock Eastlake (1836–1906), who, like his uncle and namesake (q.v.), had also become Keeper of the National Gallery.

What Beatrix's opinion was of her brother's paintings is not recorded, but to the untrained eye his *magna opera*, large landscapes of forests, rivers, and lakes, are restful and pleasing, if somewhat sombre, and curiously lacking in either human or animal content. He also maintained his interest in zoology, and in 1907 was elected a Life Fellow of the Zoological Society of London (ZSL).

When, in May 1913, Bertram, who had been living in Scotland for some years, visited his parents in Bolton Gardens, he gave them what must have been the shock of their lives. Beatrix would undoubtedly have told him about William Heelis, and how she and he had recently become engaged to be married, so Bertram decided to take this opportunity to appraise his parents of his own situation. He was married, he said, and had been so for over a decade, the wedding having taken place on 28 November 1902 in Edinburgh. His wife was Mary Welsh Scott, a former millworker from the weaving town of Hawick, Roxburghshire, in the Scottish Borders. Mary's father, ironically, in view of what was to follow, was a wine merchant in the town. The couple had set up home at Throsk House in Stirling, where Bertram pursued his career as an artist. Here they lived until the following year when Bertram bought Ashyburn, a farm near the village of Ancrum in the Scottish Borders. Bertram, according to his employee Charles Blaikie, was popular in the district. An 'exceptional employer', he gave his workmen Saturday afternoons off, despite the objections of other employers round about. Also, he and his wife hosted musical evenings and organized an annual New Year's Day football match for the villagers.[7]

Why did Bertram find it necessary to conceal the fact of his marriage from his parents? Presumably because he knew that they would have disapproved of Mary, for the same reasons that they had disapproved of Norman Warne, i.e. that Mary was of such inferior social status as to make any conjunction of the two families quite unthinkable.

When the First World War broke out in 1914 Bertram volunteered for the armed forces but was passed over, presumably because he was in a 'reserved occupation'. Farming was considered to be of such importance to the nation that farmers were exempted from military service.

On 22 June 1918, five months before the war ended, Bertram, now aged forty-six, and Charles Blaikie, then only a youth, were digging the garden at Ashyburn farm. As the pair returned to the house, having completed their task, Bertram suddenly fell dead at Blaikie's feet. J. Hamilton Hume MD signed the death certificate, having recorded the cause of death as 'cerebral haemorrhage 1 day'.[8] Beatrix, who attended the funeral, expressed her deep regret:

> I shall miss my brother sadly. We seldom met, but he wrote regularly about farming matters & we could help one another a bit, by exchange. He sent me a splendid ram last year.[9]

Bertram was buried at the parish church at Ancrum. His tombstone, in the shape of a cross, bears the simple inscription:

IN MEMORY OF
WALTER BERTRAM POTTER
OF ASHYBURN ANCRUM
THE BELOVED HUSBAND OF
MARY POTTER
BORN 14TH MARCH 1872
DIED 22ND JUNE 1918

The cerebral haemorrhage, or 'stroke', which Bertram had sustained had occurred at a relatively young age and it is prudent to enquire why. A clue which may be relevant is given by Beatrix's biographer, Linda Lear, who stated that:

> His life was marred by bouts of drinking, and his alcoholism was both recognized and tolerated charitably by his farm-hands and neighbours as 'his little weakness'.[10]

Judy Taylor, another of Beatrix's biographers, remarked that 'His years of drinking had taken their toll.'[11] And journalist Liz Taylor noted that 'His drinking was a problem and when [in his younger days] he was allowed to go off on painting trips to Birnam in Perthshire, the family hired a man to "carry his easel" and try to keep him sober.'[12] Finally, G. A. C. Binnie writes:

> Bertram became a small-time farmer and artist in Ancrum but was cut out of his father's will when he dared to marry

a Hawick wine merchant's daughter. He was over fond of his father-in-law's potions [of wine] and died prematurely in 1918.[13]

A possibility springs to mind as to how and where Bertram met Mary Scott, his wife-to-be. On 30 April 1902, seven months before Bertram married Mary, Beatrix wrote to Norman Warne to say that she was leaving London the following day for Kalemouth, Scotland, for a period of two weeks. Her brother Bertram and, of course, her parents also, would accompany her.[18] Although Beatrix gives Kalemouth as the Potters' destination, G. A. C. Binnie records that they stayed at 'Knowesouth', a mansion situated two miles to the west of the town of Jedburgh.[19] Did Bertram, during the course of the holiday, make the twelve-mile journey to Hawick, and there visit the wine merchant, run by Mary's father, in order to replenish his supplies of drink? And was he served in the shop by Mary herself; and did he fall in love with her there and then? This appears to be a distinct possibility.

The Armistice, which ended hostilities, came into effect on 11 November 1918, by which time, eleven men from the parish of Sawrey had lost their lives, and twenty-one from nearby Hawkshead. John Cannon now retired as farm manager and was replaced at Hill Top Farm by William Mackereth of Grasmere.

Beatrix maintained contact with Bertram's widow, Mary, who, she said, 'let the farm which my brother willed to her and lives very quietly with her niece'.[20] Mary outlived Bertram by twenty years. She died on 22 February 1939 and was buried in the churchyard at Ancrum in the same tomb as Bertram. Both Beatrix and William attended the funeral.

Notes

1. Linder, *The Journal of Beatrix Potter from 1881–1897*, 14 October 1892.
2. Ibid, 21–31 December 1895.
3. Beatrix to Winifrede Moore, 14 June 1897. Taylor, *Beatrix Potter's Letters*, pp. 48–9.
4. Beatrix to Winifrede Moore, 6 October 1902. Taylor, *Beatrix Potter's Letters*, p. 68.

5. Beatrix to Norman Warne, 10 May 1903. Taylor, *Beatrix Potter's Letters*, p. 75.
6. Beatrix to Norman Warne, 25 July 1905. Taylor, *Beatrix Potter's Letters*, p. 123.
7. Taylor, Liz, 'The Tale of Bertram Potter', *Weekend Scotsman*. 11 November 1978.
8. Ibid.
9. Beatrix to Millie Warne, 30 June 1918. Beatrix Potter Society Studies, in Lear, *Beatrix Potter: A Life in Nature*, p. 295.
10. Lear, *Beatrix Potter: A Life in Nature*, pp. 295–96.
11. Taylor, *Beatrix Potter: Artist, Storyteller and Countrywoman*, p. 142.
12. Taylor, Liz, 'The Tale of Bertram Potter', *The Scotsman*. 11 November 1978.
13. Binnie, G. A. C. *The Churches and Graveyards of Roxburghshire*.
14. *Drinking and Stroke Risk*. 1 January 2007. Medical University of South Carolina, USA.
15. Linder, op. cit., 1887.
16. Ibid, 1887.
17. Wayne, Howard H. 2009. *Living Longer With Heart Disease: The Non-invasive Approach That Can Save Your Life*. Los Angeles, USA: Health Information Press.
18. Beatrix to Norman Warne, 30 April 1902 and 2 May 1902. Taylor, *Beatrix Potter's Letters*, pp. 60–1.
19. Binnie, G. A. C., op. cit.
20. Beatrix to Anne Carroll Moore, 2 August 1937. Morse, *Beatrix Potter's Americans: Selected Letters*, p. 81.

CHAPTER 24

The Influence of the Reverend Hardwicke Drummond Rawnsley

BEATRIX was sixteen years old when she and her family first met the Reverend Rawnsley and his wife, Edith. That was in 1882 when the Potters had leased Wray Castle, situated on the western shore of Lake Windermere, for their summer holiday. The castle, a Victorian folly in the style of the Gothic Revival, together with the adjacent church, had been built in 1840 by retired surgeon Dr James Dawson. When Dawson died in 1875 the castle was inherited by his nephew Preston Rawnsley, who was the Reverend Rawnsley's cousin. The Potters renewed their acquaintanceship with the Rawnsleys in 1885 when they first rented Lingholm, Derwentwater, for their summer holiday.

The fact that Rawnsley was an Anglican, and a priest at that, rather than a Unitarian, in no way deterred the Potters from making a friend of him and his wife. In fact, there were several reasons for the Potters to have admired and respected him. He was energetic and industrious, qualities which led one of his parishioners to describe him as 'the most active volcano

149

in Europe'.[1] A pioneering educationalist, he founded several educational establishments designed to be accessible to the poorer classes. Also, he was concerned that the poor be provided with adequate housing and sanitation. All these qualities were, of course, entirely in accordance with the Potters' Unitarian traditions. But what endeared Beatrix to Rawnsley, above all, was his love of the Lake District and of all aspects of its traditional life.

Rawnsley was, in many ways, ahead of his time. He encouraged what today would be called sustainable farming and extolled the virtues of home-grown produce, ideas which Beatrix herself put into practice in respect of her own farms. He championed the rights of ramblers to enjoy the fells, and fought to keep open the footpaths which provided access to them. On a more sinister note, he foresaw that this part of England, the beauty of which had inspired so many of Wordsworth's poems including the one which was arguably the most famous, 'Daffodils', was in danger of despoliation by slate-carrying railways, pollution from mines, inappropriate road construction and, latterly, electric tramways. So he decided to do something about it by creating, in 1883, 'The Lake District Defence Society' (later known as 'The Friends of the Lake District') whose aims were:

> To protect the Lake District from those injurious encroachments upon its scenery which are from time to time attempted from purely commercial or speculative motives, without regard to its claims as a national recreation ground.[2]

He left Wray to become Vicar of St Kentigern's Church, Crosthwaite, near Keswick in July 1883 and, eight years later, became Honorary Canon of Carlisle Cathedral. A decade later, on 16 November 1893, Rawnsley met Miss Octavia Hill, the social reformer, and Sir Robert Hunter, Solicitor to the Commons Preservation Society – Britain's oldest national conservation body – the word 'Common' referring to common land, to found the National Trust for Places of Historic Interest and Natural

Beauty. The following year the Trust was inaugurated under The Companies Act, with Hugh Lupus Grosvenor, First Duke of Westminster, as its inaugural president, and Rawnsley as its honorary secretary, a post in which the latter continued for the remainder of his life. The Trust's first acquisition in the Lake District, made in 1902, was the Brandelhow Woods and Fell, Derwentwater, which was purchased for the sum of £6,500, and its very first life member was Beatrix's father, Mr Potter.

In October 1898 Keswick High School, one of the first co-educational schools in the country, was founded by Rawnsley.

When, in 1901, Rawnsley encouraged Beatrix to seek a publisher for her book *The Tale of Peter Rabbit*, he himself was already a published author. His *Ruskin in the English Lakes*, for example, was published in that very year. (John Ruskin, author and art critic, had died in 1900. He had been Slade Professor of Fine Art at Oxford where Rawnsley, as an undergraduate, had attended his lectures. Subsequently the two had become friends.) Other works by Rawnsley included *Lake District Sonnets* (1881), *Poems, Ballads, and Bucolics* (1890), *Notes for the Nile* (1892) – based on visits which he had made to Egypt in 1887 and 1890 – and *Harvey Goodwin, Bishop of Carlisle* (1896). Rawnsley became President of the Cumberland Nature Club in 1904 and eight years later was appointed Honorary Chaplain to King George V.

Rawnsley's wife, Edith, died in December 1916. The following year, he retired from the ministry, due to ill health, to live at Allan Bank, Grasmere, where Wordsworth had lived between 1811 and 1813. In June 1918 he married his secretary, Eleanor Simpson of Grasmere. Rawnsley died on 28 May 1920 and was buried in Crosthwaite Parish Churchyard, leaving Allan Bank to the National Trust. In his memory, Friars Crag, Lord's Island, and part of Great Wood, Derwentwater, were purchased for the Trust by public subscription. Eleanor died in 1959.

The influence of Rawnsley on Beatrix's life cannot be over-estimated and, in respect of the Lake District, this cherished cause of his became hers also. Anything that disturbed its peace and quiet was guaranteed to inflame her emotions: 'There is a beastly fly-swimming spluttering aeroplane careering up & down over Windermere; it makes a noise like 10 million bluebottles' she told Millie Warne in December 1911.[3] The following April she declared that she was 'very pleased to hear that the roof of the hydro hangar has blown in & smashed two machines'. This was a reference to the hydro-planes – fast, light motorboats, which were operating in Windermere's Bowness Bay, much to Beatrix's disgust.[4] In 1928 she referred to the 'horrible motor charabancs that have done so much to spoil the Lake District',[5] and she later complained that 'ancient footpaths' were now being used by motorcyclists.[6] However, in 1924, Beatrix finally acknowledged the arrival of the internal combustion engine by purchasing for herself a motor car, a brand new Morris Cowley. She did not drive it, however. Instead, she was driven around either by her husband William or by her chauffeur, Tommy Christie. In regard to electric power, however, this, for her, was a step too far, for it was said that

> when electricity at last came to Sawrey in 1936 … the entire village was lit up, except Hill Top and Castle Cottage, for Beatrix Potter refused to have electricity in her houses. 'But you can put it in the byres; the cows might like it,' she said.[7]

Rawnsley had imbued Beatrix with a missionary-type of zeal, not for the saving of souls though no doubt he would have been delighted if this had been the case, but for the acquisition of as much of Lakeland as possible for the National Trust. To this end, from February 1926, Beatrix was in constant communication with the Trust's Secretary, Samuel H. Hamer, concerning the possibility of certain properties and lands coming up for sale, which the Trust might wish to acquire and preserve. In June Beatrix made it clear that she proposed to bequeath Troutbeck Park Farm to the National Trust in her will. She also desired that, from henceforth, she and the Trust run the property as a partnership. To this end she strove to put Troutbeck Park onto a sound financial footing, outlining to Hamer the number of sheep which would be required to stock the land, the type and amount of fencing which would be required, and how the woodlands were to be managed.[8] That October she wrote to Hamer concerning the Trust's intention to appoint their first land agent for the Lake District. The agent, she said

> should be a superior man ... with a clear head, a good presence, presentable in London; honourably independent [and] above local politics and squabbles.[9]

When, in 1927, a strip of land on the shore of Lake Windermere was advertised for sale, and thus threatened with 'development', Beatrix responded by forwarding to American Bertha Mahony Miller, co-founder of *The Horn Book* magazine, which was devoted to children's literature, fifty signed copies of her drawings of 'Peter Rabbit', for her to sell in order that the money required to purchase the land could be raised.

Land at Tilberthwaite and Yewdale came onto the market in October 1929 and Beatrix expressed an interest 'because my great grandfather had land there and I always longed to buy it back and give it to the [National] Trust in rememberance (sic)'.[10]

The outcome was that she duly acquired the 2,500-acre Monk Coniston Estate at the head of Coniston Water, which included Yewdale, Tilberthwaite Fells, Tarn Hows, Tom Heights, and the summit of Wetherlam, most northerly of the Coniston fells, half of which she agreed to sell to the National Trust. The Trust succeeded in raising sufficient funds for the purpose and asked Beatrix if she would become managing agent of the estate on their behalf, to which she agreed.

Beatrix described, in a letter to Fanny Cooper in December 1930, how:

> I went to Coniston to Holme Ground Farm which once belonged to our great grandfather Abraham Crompton. It is a lovely spot – it was like fairyland today, with the sunshine on the craggs and snow and bracken, and hoare frost on the birch trees. The National Trust has bought the main part [of the Monk Coniston Estate]. I was able to give them Holme Ground and the wood behind it, so it is in good hands.[11]

On the Monk Coniston Estate Beatrix built a new house for her farm shepherd 'faithfully copying the style of the neighbouring farmhouse, with its cylindrical chimneys and mullion-and-transom windows'.[12] (She went on to purchase more farms in Little Langdale, Hawkshead, and Eskdale, together with cottages in and around Sawrey, which she rented to local people.) Beatrix saw her custodianship as extending not only to the properties, but also to the people who inhabited them. In February 1931, for example, she expressed concern about the dilapidated condition of the farmhouse at Yewdale, and of the poor sanitation at the National Trust's cottages at Tilberthwaite. At Ston[e]y End, Ambleside, she was appalled to learn that there were '15 people using one earth closet [toilet]'. And when her husband, William, expressed the opinion that the rents received for these cottages were 'so low they aren't worth repair', Beatrix begged to differ. 'One *has* to! [repair them],' she said firmly.[13] Rawnsley would, of course, have concurred with her sentiments absolutely.

It was not until 1933 that the Trust appointed its first land agent for Lakeland, the position being awarded to its Assistant Secretary, Bruce L. Thompson, whose duties would include the management of the Trust's portion of the Monk Coniston Estate. The appointment, however, was not to Beatrix's liking, and, in May 1938, she wrote to Donald M. Matheson who had succeeded Thompson as Assistant Secretary to express her irritation.

> Mr Thompson's usual excuse for delaying farm repairs is that he 'has no money'. Is it the policy of the National Trust to take no interest in its farms? or is it not? I have asked Mr Thompson 3 times not to buy the 'wry lock' type of netting but he seems to have no understanding about anything; and he is not learning either. If my cattle hang themselves or get lost you will have to pay for them.[14]

In October 1939, again in a letter to Matheson, she was even more scathing about Thompson, who in her opinion, did not realize the importance of preserving that which was aesthetically pleasing in the landscape:

It is useless for me to talk to him. A man cannot help having been born dull. Thompson is supercilious as well. He destroyed the finest group of oaks on Thwaite [a small estate which Beatrix had donated to the Trust], dealing with a man he had been warned against. Recently he was negociating [sic] the sale of Tilberthwaite coppice with another un-suitable man, a rough dealer in firewood.

And, as a result of Thompson's activities, 'My husband and I never drive through Coniston without vexation,' said Beatrix.[15]

Long after Rawnsley's death, Beatrix referred to him in a letter which she sent to his widow, Eleanor, to say of the latter's late husband, 'The Canon's original aim for complete preservation of as much property as possible by acquisition was the right one for the Lake District'. And she subsequently declared that despite the fact that so much of the English countryside had been 'wilfully destroyed', nonetheless she had 'tried to do my humble bit of preservation in this district'.[16] This, surely, was an understatement.

Rawnsley had been the prime mover in the creation, in the summer of 1897, of the Cumberland and Westmorland Nursing Association 'in which he and Edith never lost their interest'. This was to commemorate Queen Victoria's Diamond Jubilee.[17] He was also a member of the committee responsible for found-ing a sanatorium for sufferers from tuberculosis, which opened at Blencathra near Keswick in October 1904.[18] Beatrix, for her part, had always shown concern for the sick, and it was largely through her efforts that, in October 1914, a nurse was appointed for Sawrey and District. Declared William Heelis's great-nephew, John:

It is perhaps, not so well known that she [Beatrix] provided the first nurse's house, and [also] bought her a car.

Sixteen years later Beatrix was instrumental in establishing a trust to ensure that this nursing service would be continued. Further good works were to follow. In her time, said Beatrix, her

155

mother had 'transcribed many volumes for a Blind Association in London',[19] and, in 1921, Beatrix gave consent for six of her 'tales' to be published in Braille. In 1924, despite her failing eyesight, she took the trouble to draw her rabbit characters 'Peter' and 'Cottontail' and donate the pictures to the Invalid Children's Aid Association, to be used for its benefit.[20]

Notes

1. Nettleton, John, 2005, 'Canon Rawnsley' – Europe's 'most active volcano'! In Beatrix Potter Studies XI, Beatrix Potter Society, 2005.
2. Rawnsley, Eleanor F., *Canon Rawnsley: An Account of his Life*, p. 52.
3. Beatrix to Millie Warne, 13 December 1911. Taylor, *Beatrix Potter's Letters*, p. 192.
4. Beatrix to Harold Warne, 4 April 1912. Taylor, *Beatrix Potter's Letters*, pp. 196–7.
5. Beatrix to Marian Frazer Harris Perry, 17 December 1928. Morse, *Beatrix Potter's Americans: Selected Letters*, p. 19.
6. Beatrix to D. M. Matheson, 22 January 1935. Taylor, *Beatrix Potter's Letters*, p. 373.
7. Taylor, Willow, *Through the Pages of Life and My Encounters with Beatrix Potter*, p. 34.
8. Beatrix to S. H. Hamer, 26 June 1926. Taylor, *Beatrix Potter's Letters*, p. 296.
9. Beatrix to S. H. Hamer, 20 October 1929. Taylor, *Beatrix Potter's Letters*, p. 317.
10. Beatrix to Henry P. Coolidge, 27 October 1929. Morse, *Beatrix Potter's Americans: Selected Letters*, p. 30.
11. Beatrix to Fanny Cooper, 15 December 1930. National Trust.
12. Susan Denyer, *Beatrix Potter and her Farms*, p. 27.
13. Beatrix to S. H. Hamer, 27 February 1931. Taylor, *Beatrix Potter's Letters*, p. 342.
14. Beatrix to D. M. Matheson, 9 May 1938. Taylor, *Beatrix Potter's Letters*, p. 389.
15. Beatrix to D. M. Matheson 17 October 1939. Taylor, *Beatrix Potter's Letters*, p. 409.
16. Beatrix to John Stone, 5 June 1940. Taylor, *Beatrix Potter's Letters*, p. 416.
17. Rawnsley, Eleanor F., op. cit., p. 122–23.
18. Ibid, p. 171.
19. Beatrix to American Alexander McKay, publisher of *The Fairy Caravan*, 13 July 1938. Taylor, *Beatrix Potter's Letters*, p. 391.
20. Beatrix to Dulcie – an unidentified child – 18 April 1925. Taylor, *Beatrix Potter's Letters*, p. 292.

CHAPTER 25

Harold Warne

IF BEATRIX had thought for a moment that her relationship with her publisher, Frederick Warne & Co., would continue to be a happy and uncomplicated one, she was in for a rude awakening for, in April 1917, an extraordinary event occurred. Harold Warne, head of the publishing firm, was arrested and charged with 'Uttering a bill of exchange for £988.10s.3d, knowing it to be forged'. Harold had done this in order to finance a fishing business, left to him by his mother in her will, which was in financial difficulties, and he had drawn money from his publishing company in order to finance it. For this he was sentenced to eighteen months' imprisonment with hard labour. Fruing now took charge and, in May 1919, a new firm, Frederick Warne & Company Ltd., was registered, with himself as its new Managing Director.

Tensions between Beatrix and Harold had been brewing for some time. For example, on 18 December 1915, she had complained to Fruing about Harold's failure to send her the accounts relating to royalties for the sales of her books for the period from 1913 up to the spring of 1914:

> I think you will allow that the failure to send any statements at all is a trial of patience; and the overlapping and

unpunctuality had begun *long* before the war. If the matter of the accounts is not gone into satisfactorily by the end of January, I shall have to take some steps about it ... [1]

Lesser mortals than Beatrix might have thrown up their hands in despair, not only at this blow to the prestige of Warne, but also because the firm owed her money. But Beatrix was made of sterner stuff and resolved to do all in her power to retrieve the situation. She would remain loyal to her publisher and she would demonstrate her loyalty by presenting Warne with her *Appley Dapply's Nursery Rhymes*, which was published in October 1917, in good time for Christmas, together with two new painting books. However, her assistance would not be unconditional, as she made clear in a letter to Fruing:

> I want to say it must be clearly understood that 'H' [Harold] never meddles again. I bear him no grudge, but I know & remember what a trial he has been to me for many years.[2]

And Warne, for its part, compensated her, as their largest creditor, with an allocation of a gift of shares in the company. Finally, on 11 March 1920, a relieved Beatrix was delighted to tell Fruing, 'I am very glad indeed that the old firm is doing so well and righting itself.'[3] When Fruing died in February 1928, aged sixty-six, he was succeeded as managing director by Arthur Stephens, his brother-in-law.

So here is an example of Beatrix reflecting the tenacity and obstinacy of her Lancastrian ancestors, especially that of the Cromptons, and what she described as 'the strength that comes from the hills', by fighting to preserve both her own interests, and those of Frederick Warne & Company Ltd.

Notes

1. Beatrix to Fruing Warne, 18 December 1915. Taylor, *Beatrix Potter's Letters*, p. 222.
2. Beatrix to Fruing Warne, 4 May 1918. Taylor, *Beatrix Potter's Letters*, p. 247.
3. Beatrix to Fruing Warne, 11 March 1920. Taylor, *Beatrix Potter's Letters*, p. 261.

CHAPTER 26

The Fairy Caravan

A PERSON reading *The Fairy Caravan* who knew nothing about Beatrix Potter might be forgiven for thinking that this was no more than an entirely fictional story. However, in the book Beatrix reveals many aspects of her own character. The story evolved in the following way. It began life as the *Tale of Tuppenny*, which was written in 1903, but never published. Twenty-six years later, in 1929, the story was rewritten and became Chapter 1 of *The Fairy Caravan*.

It was Beatrix's 'Highland nurse girl', Anne Mackenzie, who had first introduced her to the concept of fairies. And it was when she was walking alone near Troutbeck in the Lake District that the idea of the story first came to her:

> In a soft muddy spot on the old drove road I had found a multitude of un-shod footprints, much too small for horses' footmarks, much too round for deer or sheep. I wondered were they foot marks of a troupe of fairy riders ... The finding of those little fairy foot steps on the old drove road first made me aware of the Fairy Caravan.[1] (Beatrix is known to have visited Troutbeck in August 1895).

However, the characters in the story are principally little creatures from the animal kingdom which bear no relationship to

159

fairies, other than that they possess magical properties. Tuppenny the guinea pig, is described as 'miserable and ill-used' and 'of dilapidated appearance', who came from a town called Marmalade (in the Land of Green Ginger) which was inhabited entirely by other guinea pigs. Tuppenny became a figure of fun when his fellow guinea pigs treated him with a hair stimulant which made his hair grow uncontrollably. He therefore decided to run away to the countryside where he came across Alexander & William's Circus, which travelled around in a two-wheeled cart and a four-wheeled caravan. Its members included Jane Ferret, Iky Shepster the starling, Paddy Pig, Pony Billy and Xarifa the dormouse. The animals were all in miniature, as were the caravan and cart. Incidentally, Beatrix, in her journal, describes visiting the real circus on several occasions, both in Scotland and in the Lake District. For example, her visit to Ginnet's Travelling Circus at Ambleside on 16 April 1885, was, she said 'very good ...'.

Tuppeny was welcomed by members of the circus who led him to the fire where he could warm his cold and wet body and gave him 'a mug of hot balm tea and a baked apple', with the result that 'he was much comforted by the warmth of the fire and by their kindness'. The outcome was that he joined the circus. Did Beatrix, as a child, long to do likewise? Perhaps so. The circus travelled at night, each of its members carrying fern seeds in their pocket which made them invisible to 'the big folk', i.e. human beings. Circus animals showed great concern for each other. For example, when Pony Billy was captured by the big folk and taken to the pound, it was Sandy the dog who arranged for Blacksmith Mettle, a dog, to release the padlock and set him free.

When Beatrix was writing about a subject which she was passionate about, in this case the countryside, her prose was equal to the occasion, as, in this instance, was her knowledge of plants and the seasons of the year. For example:

The caravan wandered along green ways. Primroses were peeping out at the edge of the coppice; the oak showed a tinge of gold; the wild cherry trees were snow-white with

160

blossom. Beech trees and sycamores were bursting into leaf; only the ash trees remained bare as in mid-winter. The ash is the last to don her green gown, and the first to lose her yellow leaves; a short-lived summer lady.

In Chapter 7 Xarifa reminisces about 'Bird's Place', the garden of an old manor house in Hertfordshire which she remembered from her childhood. It was a paradise where 'birds and butter-flies and flowers lived undisturbed in that pleasant green wilderness that had once been a garden'. Surely here Beatrix is living vicariously through Xarifa and imagining herself to be in the garden of Camfield, the Hertfordshire home of her grand-parents, Edmund and Jessie Potter, whom she used to visit as a child.

In Chapter 14 the author describes the approach of Christmas and, on Christmas Eve, a fall of snow. There is:

a very small spruce, a little Christmas tree some four foot high. As the night grew darker – the branches of this little tree became all tipped with light, and wreathed with icicles and chains of frost.

Small voices and music began to mingle with the sound of the water [from the nearby stream]. Up by the snowy banks, from the wood and from the meadow beyond, tripped scores of little shadowy creatures, advancing from the darkness into the light. They trod a circle on the snow around the Christmas tree, dancing gaily hand-in-hands. [and then suddenly] The lights on the Christmas tree quivered, and went out. All was darkness and silence. 'I'm afraid the Christmas picnic was only a dream ...'

Surely this is Beatrix, again as a child, dreaming of having a 'proper' Christmas, rather than a Unitarian-style one. She herself appears in Chapter 17, when Fran, a collie dog, enquires saucily, 'Does Mistress Heelis really ever take her clogs [wooden-soled shoes with leather uppers] off? I thought she went to bed in

161

them?' Beatrix wore clogs when she went about her farming duties.

The final chapter contains a lament for an ancient oak tree, inhabited for many hundreds of years by a fairy, which the 'Surveyor of the District Council' who had 'no sentiment and no respect, either for fairies or for oaks' decreed must be cut down. This is Beatrix the conservationist and lover of all things traditional speaking.

Beatrix was disinclined to allow *The Fairy Caravan* to be published in England, even by Frederick Warne, as the story was 'too personal – too autobiographical'.[2] Was Beatrix afraid that her English readers would guess that she, like Tuppence, had considered herself to be 'miserable and ill-used', [at Bolton Gardens] and had been desperate to escape to a new life in a better place [the Lake District]? The proposition is a likely one. On the other hand, were the chapters of the book to be 'printed in an American journal' and were they to look 'silly in print' and be 'considered foolishness', then 'I needn't see them at all'. Any embarrassment would therefore be avoided, for Americans were 'not afraid of being laughed at for [being] sentimental'.[3]

The outcome was that *The Fairy Caravan*, which Beatrix dedicated to Henry Parsons Coolidge from Boston, USA, who, as a thirteen-year-old boy, had visited her in the Lake District with his mother in the summer of 1927, was published in the USA in October 1929 by David McKay of Philadelphia, and its sequel, *Sister Anne*, featuring the infamous and seven-times married 'Baron Bluebeard', in December 1932. It was not until 1952 that *The Fairy Caravan* was finally published in England by Frederick Warne.

Notes

1. Linder, *A History of the Writings of Beatrix Potter*, p. 293.
2. Beatrix to Bertha Mahony Miller, 20 November 1942. Morse, *Beatrix Potter's Americans: Selected Letters*, p. 192.
3. Beatrix to Mrs J. Templeman Coolidge, 30 September 1927. Taylor, *Beatrix Potter's Letters*, p. 306.

CHAPTER 27

Sheep: Joseph Moscrop

AS MIGHT be expected, the Reverend Rawnsley, who had the proverbial finger in every pie where Lakeland matters were concerned, had a hand in the creation of the Herdwick Sheep Association when, in 1899, his son Noel, archaeologist, horticulturalist and traveller, and S. D. Stanley Dodgson, land agent of Tarnbank, Cockermouth, called a meeting of Herdwick sheep breeders at Keswick, where Rawnsley senior was elected to the chair.[1] More than half a century earlier, however, in 1844, the West Cumberland Fell Dales Sheep Association had been created with an annual show and sale, whereby breeders could 'get access to fell tups (rams, in this case, of the best quality), either to be bought or to be hired'.[2] Twenty years later, in 1864, the Fell Dales Association for the Improvement of Herdwick Sheep was created with the aim of producing a hardy breed suitable for 'prospering at the fell'.[3]

To move forward again to 1899, the aims of the Herdwick Sheep Association, as articulated by Noel Rawnsley, included improving and maintaining the Herdwick as a distinct breed; publicizing the breed, and advertising its hardy characteristics and the excellent quality of its mutton; specifying the characteristics to be 'desired in a typical Herdwick', and ensuring that a special class for Herdwicks existed at shows held, not just locally, but also further afield.[4]

In 1911 the Reverend Rawnsley published *By Fell and Dale in the English Lakes* which contains a chapter entitled 'A Crack about Herdwick Sheep'. (Sheep 'cracking' – the word is derived from the Norse, meaning that the sheep are following one another briskly across the fell.)[5] This covered all aspects of the breed and its management, including shearing (clipping), sheep-dogs, dipping and the prevention of disease, and how to cope with snowy conditions. Rawnsley commented on the remarkable 'homing instincts' of Herdwicks which

> appear to know their bounds almost to a yard upon the mountain-side [even] though there are no walls or a fence to prevent them straying beyond their pastures.[6]

He also describes Herdwick mutton as 'the sweetest of its kind in Great Britain'. He tells how the sheep are earmarked for identification, the mark being recorded in the 'Flock Book', the first of which, *The Shepherd's Book or Guide*, was created by J. Walker of Martindale in the year 1817.[7]

July is clipping time when 'there are perhaps 600–1,200 sheep to be clipped and the best hand at clipping cannot clip more than seventy or eighty in a day'. Therefore, neighbours come to the rescue, 'stream in from far and near, over hill and dale, with their clipping clothes and their shears in a bundle under their arms'. And by 8pm, when the day's work is done,

> there is a good supper and a shepherd's song or two, perhaps a bit of a dance with the girls of the farm, to bring the clipping to an end.[8]

The wool of the Herdwicks, said Rawnsley, was made into 'great coats' and 'fellside jackets and trousers' for the farmers, together with 'cloths, frieze rugs [of heavy, napped wool], and plaids and blankets'. So successful were the efforts of Rawnsley and others that by the early twentieth century there were an estimated half a million Herdwick sheep on the Lakeland fells.[9]

As Beatrix explained, Herdwick sheep with their '*hard* [i.e. resilient] water-proof jackets, were 'the only sort that can thrive on the high fells'.[10] However:

> The Herdwick breed was under threat as more farmers turned to keeping breeds with softer fleeces and plumper lambs in response to changing demands from the woollen and meat industries. [In fact] the demand for their wool almost ceased when linoleum came in and carpets went out of fashion.'[11] (This was from the beginning of the twentieth century onwards.)

In 1923 Beatrix acquired Troutbeck Park Farm, situated to the north of Windermere at the head of the Troutbeck Valley, and consisting of almost 2,000 acres. It was here, with the aid of local shepherd Tom Storey, that she attempted to put Rawnsley's ideas into practice by establishing a flock of 1,000 or so 'purebred heafed Herdwicks' ('heafed' meaning that they graze an area of unfenced land, from which they do not stray). And from 1926 she employed Joseph Moscrop ('Joe'), an experienced shepherd from the Scottish Borders, to help Storey with the lambing. (Joe also worked for his cousin, John-Willie Beaty of Saughtrees, near the Borders town of Newcastleton in Roxburghshire.)

(There were other female sheep farmers and breeders in Lakeland, apart from Beatrix, but they were few and far between. They included Mrs Leck of Troutbeck, and, following the death of her husband, Mrs Rawlings of The Hollins, Ennerdale.[12] Another was Mrs Huck of Adamthwaite near Ravenstonedale. She was a member of the Rough Fell Sheep Breeders' Association, founded in November 1926 and located in the Kendal area, and she and her son bred sheep for a Mr T. Sedgwick of Thwaite Farm, Howgill.)[13]

In 1927, with the retirement of farm manager William Makereth, Beatrix asked Tom Storey if he would relocate from Troutbeck

165

Park Farm to Hill Top Farm, where it was her intention to breed Herdwick sheep for showing. This she did so successfully that her sheep subsequently won prizes at shows, both locally and as far afield as Keswick, Ennerdale, Eskdale, and Loweswater. Beatrix's body-language – as when, in the presence of Tom Storey and of her ewe, 'Water Lily', she held aloft a card on which were written the words 'SPECIAL PRIZE' – indicates nothing less than unmitigated pleasure coupled, no doubt, with a smattering of pride. She had succeeded in a world dominated by some of the hardiest and most independent-minded men in the land and, not only that, she had proved her worth amongst them.

The strength of Beatrix's admiration and enthusiasm for her sheep is revealed by her in Chapter 10 of *The Fairy Caravan*. Here Beatrix herself appears as 'Mistress Heelis', the owner of a flock of Herdwick sheep which, unlike 'the silly Southron [Southern English] sheep', are able to find their way around with no need of 'guide, nor star, nor compass ...'. Herdwick sheep, wrote Beatrix, were even now as 'wild and free' as when the 'stone-men' [Stone Age men] inhabited the land, and as

> untamed as when the Norsemen named our grassings [hill pastures] in their stride. On through the fleeting centuries, when fresh blood came from Iceland, Spain, or Scotland – stubborn, unchanged, UNBEATEN – we have held the stony waste. Hold the proud ancient heritage of our Herdwick sheep.

Lambs, however, are described by Beatrix as being 'thoughtless and giddy'. Lady Ulla Hyde Parker was highly impressed with Beatrix's knowledge, and described her as

> an expert on sheep farming, sheep and sheepdogs. She knew intimately every acre we passed and she also understood the upkeep of the land, the farm houses and farm buildings.

Ulla also said that Beatrix and her shepherds 'understood one another', and 'knew the faces of their sheep individually', much to her amazement.[14]

In view of what has been said, the following incident, involving Beatrix, may at first sight appear somewhat shocking. In 1982 Elizabeth Battrick, author of *The Real World of Beatrix Potter* (published in 1983), visited the Lake District where she met and interviewed Beatrix's former shepherd.[15] Storey told her how, on one occasion, Beatrix requested his help, saying,

> 'Storey, the next lamb that dies, could you cut its head off me and skin it back to the shoulder?' He did as she asked. The next time he came down the lane to look at a sheep he saw her sitting on a stone in the field, sketching the head which was fastened to the wall.[16]

Consultant Psychiatrist Dr Cornelis de Wet is of the opinion that:

> As a prizewinning Herdwick sheep breeder (and Show Judge), Beatrix Potter must have had an acute appreciation of the anatomical features and dimensions of Herdwick sheep, and she must have found the appearance of specific individuals in the flock particularly pleasing. It does not strike me as unusual that, upon the death of a particular lamb, she may have wanted to have the lamb's head mounted on a wall in order to illustrate its qualities in the kind of artistic detail for which she has become so known.[17]

This opinion is shared by independent researcher and reviewer, Dr Stuart Hannabuss, who says of Beatrix:

> It is so easy, isn't it, to attribute sentimental feelings (towards nature, towards animals) to an author-illustrator who produced Squirrel Nutkin and Peter Rabbit. Even there, however (think of Peter's near-death experience, when pursued by Mr McGregor, brandishing a rake; Little Pig Robinson, who

was nearly cooked in a pot by Captain Barnabas Butcher, and Mr Tod, with his murderous intentions towards Jemima Puddle-duck), she is quite unsentimental, and many critics and writers in the tourist industry play that side down.

Looking at her later life and what we know of her attitudes, and accepting that Lakeland farming life was hard and often cruel, I am not surprised that she would have been entirely pragmatic about dead animals or the death of several lambs in every lambing season. Linking that with the scrupulous objectivity of, say, her illustrative work on fungi (dating from early years), and her interest (as an amateur scientist) in flora and fauna, I would interpret her plan to draw a dead lamb much as she would have drawn a dead butterfly or moth, mouse or vole.

Perhaps her intention to pin up a skull for drawing might have arisen too from the infirmities of age – deteriorating eyesight, increasing difficulty with arm and finger movement, and also from a need to display it in the brightest available light.[18]

In regard to her artwork, however, the results appear to indicate that sheep were not a favourite subject for Beatrix.

Anthony 'Tant' Benson, who replaced Tom Storey as shepherd at Troutbeck in 1927, describes how Beatrix's love of her sheep also extended to her sheepdogs:

> When the farm dogs reached a good age and were no longer able to work, they were all pensioned off and she had a proper kennel built for them. And every time she visited Troutbeck [Park] Farm that would be the first place she would go to – them old dogs. Some folks has them put down, but no, she would keep them. There were 14 dogs there at one time.[19]

Willow Taylor declared that Beatrix wore 'long tweed skirts and jackets made from her own Herdwick sheep's wool'. In addition, said Willow, she attired herself in:

an old felt hat in winter and a straw hat in summer. We never saw her in a light dress, even in very hot weather. She had her clogs made by a local shoemaker in Hawkshead – Charlie Brown. When it was raining [she] threw an old sack around her shoulders printed with the name 'BIBBY'S, the firm which produced animal feeds. One wet day, walking between Near and Far Sawrey, she was mistaken for a tramp.[20]

Beatrix once described the clothing she was obliged to wear as a child at Bolton Gardens as being

absurdly uncomfortable; white pique starched frocks just like Tenniel's 'Alice in Wonderland', and cotton stockings striped round and round like a zebra's legs.[21]

But now, as an independent person, she was free to dress precisely as she chose.

To Beatrix Joseph Moscrop was far more than a mere employee. Her letters to him are, in the main, full of joy and warmth. She gives him news of the weather, the harvest, her livestock, the health of herself and of her husband, and tells him that she eagerly anticipates his next visit: 'I shall be very glad to see you again at lambing time.'[22] 'It wouldn't be like lambing time without Joseph and *his* dog,'[23] and, 'It is always a pleasure to see the swallows again and Joseph's smile.'[24] In a letter to Nancy Dean, granddaughter of Bertha Mahony Miller, she says of Joe, 'He is wonderful with lambs and dogs.'[25] And yet, as she negotiates with him what his wages are to be, her business sense does not for a minute desert her as she attempts to drive a hard bargain. Such was the empathy between Beatrix and Joe that he became her confidant. For example, in 1931, she told him that her mother, Mrs Potter, now aged ninety-one,

has never exerted herself to work, in her life. I would rather keep going till I drop – early or late – never mind what the work is, so long as it is useful and well done.[26]

169

Following the death of King George V, on 20 January 1936, Beatrix told Joe:

> It has been a sad time. [but] There is one reflection that is comforting – don't you think it is to the credit of human nature that a plain honest – not very clever man should have gained so much love and respect? He has set a good and noble example and it has made an impression. [27]

King George was succeeded by Edward VIII, formerly Prince of Wales, whose abdication less than a year later was greeted by Beatrix with disgust.

One of the last letters ever written by Beatrix was to her faithful shepherd, Joe:

> I write a line to shake you by the hand, our friendship has been entirely pleasant. I am very ill with bronchitis. Best wishes for the New Year. Beatrix Heelis. [28]

Beatrix's love of Lakeland and of her sheep and sheepdogs, positively exudes from her writings.

> I loved to wander on the Troutbeck fell. Sometimes I had with me an old sheepdog, Nip, or Fly; more often I went alone. But never lonely. There was company of gentle sheep, and wild flowers and singing waters. [29]

And in the words of Willow Taylor, another 'favourite place' where she 'could be alone was in the little Jesus Church[30] in Troutbeck, where she could sit quietly and hear only the bleating of the sheep'. [31]

In 1924 Beatrix had achieved the rare distinction, for a woman, of becoming a member of the Herdwick Sheep Breeders' Association. Every year she won top prizes for her Herdwicks, and in March 1943 she was voted president-elect of the association for the following year. Sadly, however, she did not live to take up the post. Her achievements were even more remarkable in that she was forced to battle constantly against her own ill health and failing eyesight and, occasionally, against male prejudice, so much being evident in a letter which she wrote to Millie Warne, concerning the building alterations to Hill Top:

> I had rather a row with the plumber – or perhaps I ought to say I lost my temper! If he won't take orders from a lady I may pack him off and get [another] one from Kendal.[32]

Notes

1. Brown, *Herdwicks: Herdwick Sheep and the English Lake District*, p. 23.
2. Ibid, p. 14.
3. Ibid, p. 17.
4. Ibid, p. 24.
5. Rawnsley, Hardwicke, *By Fell and Dale in the English Lakes*, p. 70.
6. Ibid, pp. 50–1.
7. Ibid, p. 54.
8. Ibid, pp. 60–1.
9. Brown, op. cit., p. 25.
10. Beatrix to Bertha Mahony Miller, 18 August 1943. Morse, *Beatrix Potter's Americans: Selected Letters*, p. 198.
11. Beatrix to Bertha Mahony Miller, 18 August 1943. Morse, *Beatrix Potter's Americans: Selected Letters*, p. 198.
12. Information kindly supplied by Geoff Brown, and by the Cumbrian and Kendal Record Offices.
13. Cumbria Record Office, *Flock Book, Rough Sheep Breeders' Association Flock Book, 1927.*
14. Hyde Parker, *Cousin Beatie: a Memory of Beatrix Potter*, p. 16.
15. Battrick, *The Real World of Beatrix Potter*, p. 2.
16. Ibid, p. 55.
17. Dr Cornelis de Wet, Consultant Psychiatrist, Poole, Dorset, UK to Dr Andrew Norman, 7 March 2012.
18. Dr Stuart Hannabuss to Dr Andrew Norman, 19 March 2012.
19. Taylor, *Beatrix Potter's Farming Friendship: Lake District letters to Joseph Moscrop 1926–1943.*
20. Taylor, Willow. *Through the Pages of Life and My Encounters with Beatrix Potter*, p. 23.
21. 'Roots of the Peter Rabbit Tales'. *The Horn Book*, May 1929, Appendix.
22. Beatrix to Joseph Moscrop, 23 January 1932. Taylor, *Beatrix Potter's Letters*, p. 345.

23. Beatrix to Joseph Moscrop, 31 January 1936. Taylor, *Beatrix Potter's Letters*, p. 374.
24. Beatrix to Joseph Moscrop, 11 March 1942. Taylor, *Beatrix Potter's Farming Friendship: Lake District letters to Joseph Moscrop 1926–1943*, p. 79.
25. Beatrix to Nancy Dean, 30 July 1940. Taylor, *Beatrix Potter's Letters*, p. 421.
26. Beatrix to Joseph Moscrop, 15 January 1931. Taylor, *Beatrix Potter's Letters*, pp. 337–8.
27. Beatrix to Joseph Moscrop, 31 January 1936. Taylor, *Beatrix Potter's Letters*, p. 374.
28. Beatrix to Joseph Moscrop, 13 December 1943. Taylor, *Beatrix Potter's Letters*, p. 465.
29. Lane, *The Tale of Beatrix Potter*, p. 147.
30. Jesus Church, Troutbeck.
31. Taylor, Willow, op. cit., p. 93.
32. Beatrix to Millie Warne, in Lane, *The Tale of Beatrix Potter*, pp. 89–90.

CHAPTER 28

Another War

IN DECEMBER 1935, the year after Adolf Hitler came to power in Nazi Germany, Beatrix declared, 'If that wretched League does not drag this country into war it will be a wonder and a mercy.'[1] This was a reference to the League of Nations, founded in 1919, one of whose aims, paradoxically in view of Beatrix's comment, was to promote international disarmament.

In October 1938 Beatrix described Hitler, the Führer of Nazi Germany, as:

> a brutal raving lunatic. I could not understand a word of his clipped rapid German; but the ranting note and the smiling face in the telegraphed photographs [which appeared in the newspapers] are not sane. If [British Prime Minister] Mr Chamberlain believes in his promises he must be an incurable optimist. [Whilst she hoped that] Perhaps a better, more wise world may emerge ... [nonetheless] I have not much faith in Mr Chamberlain ...[2]

On 18 March 1939 Beatrix enquired, in a letter to Caroline Clark, 'What next? Has Franco also made a fool of Mr Chamberlain?' This was a reference to Spanish nationalist revolutionary General Francisco Franco who was about to achieve victory in the Spanish Civil War. And later in the same letter Beatrix declares, 'It is not Chamberlain's failure to save C. slovakia [Czechoslovakia] that is wrong; it is his density and smug satisfaction that is so hopeless. He does not seem ashamed at having been blind & wrong.'[3] Here, Beatrix was referring to Prime Minister Neville Chamberlain, vis-à-vis the German invasion of Czechoslovakia, which had occurred three days earlier on 15 March.

On 3 September 1939 Britain declared war on Germany, following that country's invasion of Poland. Beatrix's husband, William, received his call-up papers, but was rejected on the grounds that his health was 'only Grade 3'. He therefore served on the War Agricultural Executive Committee, one of which was created for each county in England and Wales and whose task it was to ensure the maximization of home food production, as a reserve policeman.

Late in 1939 Beatrix performed an extraordinary *volte face* in respect of Hill Top when she offered her precious retreat as accommodation to Lady Ulla Hyde Parker, her husband Sir William, their children Richard, aged two, and infant Elizabeth, and their nanny. Beatrix's reasons for doing so were twofold: the Hyde Parkers' home, Melford Hall in Suffolk, had been requisitioned by the military, and Sir William had been severely injured in a road traffic accident.

When the Hyde Parker family arrived, said Ulla, and Beatrix saw baby Elizabeth for the first time, as she lay on a shawl on the dining room table of Castle Cottage, she

> looked and looked at her, and as she gazed her eyes shone as if tears were about to break through. She drew herself up to regain her usual composure and then uttered these words . . . 'Now a baby is really sitting here on my table. Oh, something I did long for.' And I realized that perhaps the dearest wish of her life had bypassed her. That she would have loved to have children, I now knew.[4]

In the coming months Ulla would get to know Beatrix well and, as a result, make some extremely insightful observations about her. Beatrix, said Ulla, 'did not invite friendships', even with 'people whom she had known for years. Yet she was an excellent judge of character'.[5] She 'had a presence which commanded respect' and 'knows what values she upholds and stands for'. But Ulla wondered whether 'such qualities' were only to be found 'in people who have suffered for their strong individuality'.[6] Beatrix 'did not express her feelings and emotions except in her art and writings and ... she was not therefore demonstrative in any sense of the word',[7] continued Ulla, but omitted to say, however, that the former also expressed her feelings by her *deeds* – as now, when she offered hospitality to the Hyde Parker family in distress.

During her sojourn at Hill Top, Ulla was also able to observe how Beatrix behaved in the presence of children:

> She who understood so well how to stir a child's imagination seemed rather shy of them. She knew a child from within, but how to catch their interest eluded her, and she realized this and stayed somewhat silent in their presence.[8]

But when Ulla decided to hold 'a proper old-world Christmas' at Hill Top, Beatrix 'was delighted' and entered into the spirit of the occasion by presenting Richard with a 'colourful wooden toy caravan complete with horse', and his sister Elizabeth with a 'marmalade cat'.[9]

Willow Taylor saw Beatrix interacting, or more strictly speaking, failing to interact with the children of Sawrey, and with the Girl Guides who held their annual camp on Beatrix's land. Willow went so far as to say that Beatrix 'truly did not understand children. I doubt whether she had ever played a child's game in her life, because she had no childhood friends'.[10]

On 5 June 1940 Beatrix expressed her exasperation to the American Anne Carroll Moore, author and Superintendent of Children's Work at the New York Public Library who, in the summer of 1921, had been the first of many visitors from the USA to visit her at Sawrey, at the apparent failure of the latter's country to support the Allied war effort. Even if America did not enter the European war on the side of the Allies, then 'surely

USA might have sent us aeroplanes and guns ...' with which to prosecute it.[11] That September, Beatrix declared, 'The cruelty of the destruction of working class homes is horrible.' This was a reference to German bombing raids on London and other towns and cities in Britain.[12] On 10 October the Potters' former home, No. 2 Bolton Gardens, which had been Beatrix's principal residence for the first forty-seven years of her life, was destroyed by enemy bombing, as were some adjoining properties in the road. But Beatrix had no regrets about the fate of what she described as her 'unloved birthplace' – rather the opposite. 'I am rather pleased to hear it is no more,' she said.[13]

In June 1941 Beatrix demonstrated her astuteness in regard to foreign affairs when she said, 'Russia could stop Hitler if she took the oil wells [i.e. of Romania] and the Danube ports with that intention.'[14] The following month she was anxious about the possibility of a German invasion, and she described how Britain was attempting to prepare for it, if the worst came to the worst, 'We don't know what to think – there are plenty of men in readiness and barricades going up at crossroads and corners,' she said.[15] However, 'the spirit of the people is wonderful, magnificent.'[16]

On Christmas Eve 1940 Beatrix declared 'Nobody here doubts. We have *got to win*! It will be a slow and painful task.'[17] But in April 1941, when there had been German bombers 'overhead all night long', she was in a more sombre frame of mind.[18] In December 1941 Beatrix's husband William, by then aged seventy, retired from the Home Guard, but, said Beatrix, he 'still keeps his policeman's helmet and big boots'.[19]

On the 8th, the day after the Japanese attack on Pearl Harbor, Hawaii, Headquarters of the US Pacific Fleet, the USA declared war on Japan. On 11 December, Hitler and Mussolini declared war on the USA, which now became involved in the war in Europe. On 31 January 1942 a delighted Beatrix wrote to Anne Carroll Moore to say, 'Your country is truly in the war at last! How glad we are to know the American troops are in Ulster!'[20] However, she was under no illusion and declared the following November in a letter to American Bertha Mahony Miller, that

'There will be some severe fighting yet, but the war seems to have taken the right turn at last.'[21] Ten days later, she told Bertha:

> It is very hard work, but I am still managing 2 sheep farms and the small home farm, and a tractor outfit. I cannot work with my own hands now, like the last war, but I'll do my bit till I drop – and enjoy it![22]

In early January 1943 Beatrix wrote to Joseph Moscrop: 'The war news is cheering; it really seems as though the Germans are getting the lesson they have deserved, after their beastly cruelty to other nations.'[23] Later that month she complained that 'the French have double-crossed us the whole time; it is incomprehensible how anyone can countenance Vichy [the government of France from July 1940 to August 1944, which not only collaborated with the Germans, but actually took up arms against the Allies]'.[24]

In August 1943 Beatrix told Bertha Mahony Miller that she had reservations about America's future intentions:

> They say they are winning the war for *us* [but] It's to be hoped *they* don't expect to dictate the terms of peace. Not like the last time [as happened at the conclusion of the First World War].[25]

In the same month she wrote to Bertha once again, to say that although she was at present confined to bed with bronchitis nevertheless she intended 'to do a bit more active work yet – and anyhow I have survived to see Hitler beaten past hope of recovery'![26] On the last day of November Beatrix wrote to Anne Carroll Moore to say 'May next year bring peace and relief to a very wicked harassed world ...'[27]

Notes

1. Beatrix to Helen Dean Fish, 15 December 1935. Morse, *Beatrix Potter's Americans: Selected Letters*, p. 69.
2. Beatrix to Marian Frazer Harris Perry, 4 October 1938. Taylor, *Beatrix Potter's Letters*, pp. 392–93.
3. Beatrix to Caroline Clark, 18 March 1939, National Trust.

4. Hyde Parker, *Cousin Beatie: a Memory of Beatrix Potter*, p. 30.
5. Ibid, p. 19.
6. Ibid, p. 15.
7. Ibid, p. 30.
8. Ibid, p. 34.
9. Ibid, pp. 33–4.
10. Taylor, Willow, *Through the Pages of Life and My Encounters with Beatrix Potter*, p. 25.
11. Beatrix to Anne Carroll Moore, 5 June 1940. Morse, *Beatrix Potter's Americans: Selected Letters*, p. 108.
12. Beatrix to Betty and Richard Stevens, 19 September 1940. Morse, *Beatrix Potter's Americans: Selected Letters*, p. 123.
13. *The Horn Book*, May 1929. In Morse, *Beatrix Potter's Americans: Selected Letters*, p. 213.
14. Beatrix to Marian Frazer Harris Perry, 29 June 1940. Morse, *Beatrix Potter's Americans: Selected Letters*, p. 113.
15. Beatrix to Anne Carroll Moore, 11 July 1940. Morse, *Beatrix Potter's Americans: Selected Letters*, p. 115.
16. Beatrix to Bertha Mahony Miller, 11 October 1940. Morse, *Beatrix Potter's Americans: Selected Letters*, p. 145.
17. Beatrix to Marian Frazer Harris Perry, 24 December 1940. Morse, *Beatrix Potter's Americans: Selected Letters*, p. 147.
18. Beatrix to Arthur Stephens, 19 April 1951. Taylor, *Beatrix Potter's Letters*, p. 427.
19. Beatrix to Mrs J. Templeman Coolidge, 12 February 1942. Morse, *Beatrix Potter's Americans: Selected Letters*, p. 168.
20. Beatrix to Anne Carroll Moore, 31 January 1942. Morse, *Beatrix Potter's Americans: Selected Letters*, p. 165.
21. Beatrix to Bertha Mahony Miller, 10 November 1942. Morse, *Beatrix Potter's Americans: Selected Letters*, p. 186.
22. Beatrix to Bertha Mahony Miller, 20 November 1942. Morse, *Beatrix Potter's Americans: Selected Letters*, p. 192.
23. Beatrix to Joseph Moscrop, 8 January 1943. Taylor, *Beatrix Potter's Farming Friendship: Lake District letters to Joseph Moscrop 1926–1943*, p. 83.)
24. Beatrix to Marian Frazer Harris Perry, 23 January 1943. Morse, *Beatrix Potter's Americans: Selected Letters*, p. 194.
25. Beatrix to Bertha Mahony Miller, 18 August 1943. Taylor, *Beatrix Potter's Letters*, pp. 198–99.
26. Beatrix to Bertha Mahony Miller, 5 November 1943. Morse, *Beatrix Potter's Americans: Selected Letters*, p. 202.
27. Beatrix to Anne Carroll Moore, 30 November 1943. Morse, *Beatrix Potter's Americans: Selected Letters*, p. 204.

CHAPTER 29

The Death of Beatrix

BEATRIX died on the night of 22 December 1943 at Castle Cottage. She was seventy-seven. The cause of death, certified by A. Brownlee MB, was given as 'acute bronchitis, myocarditis, and carcinoma of the uterus'. Shortly before her death she had summoned her shepherd, Tom Storey, to her bedside and requested that he stay on and manage the farm for William after her departure. This he agreed to do.

Willow Taylor, speaking of Sawrey, declared that:

> When someone in the village community died, it was the normal practice at that time for local people to draw their curtains while the coffin was brought through the village to the church, but there was no service in church for Mrs Heelis.[1]

Instead, her body was taken to Blackpool on the Lancashire coast and cremated at a private ceremony. She had requested that there be 'No mourning, no flowers, and no letters, please'. Why Blackpool? Simply because, given that Beatrix had decided to be cremated, this was the crematorium which was nearest to Sawrey. Her ashes were scattered on her beloved Fells by Storey. He agreed to keep the location at which this was done secret.

179

The terms of Beatrix's will ensured that, even after her death, those for whom she had been responsible during her lifetime would continue to be treated fairly, for she stipulated that 'My house property shall continue to be let at moderate rents to the same class of tenants as heretofore, and ... my farms shall be let at moderate rents to good tenants.'[2] Her will also decreed that her favourite pieces of furniture were to be retained at Hill Top Farm and also that 'No old horse or worn out dog [was] to be sold; [it was] either [to be] given to a really trustworthy person or put down'. She left in excess of 4,000 acres of Lakeland to the National Trust, including fifteen farms, numerous cottages and some quarries. This was augmented on William's death when he, in turn, left to that organization, those farms which he had held in trust for his lifetime, together with a further 258 acres of farmland. Finally, Beatrix stipulated that on those of her farms where the flocks were fell-going, the sheep should continue to be 'of the pure Herdwick breed'.[3]

The Second World War officially ended in Europe on 8 May 1945. With the loss of Beatrix, William was broken-hearted. He died in a nursing home in York on 4 August at the age of seventy-three.[4] His body was cremated. Ten days later, Japan officially surrendered to the Allies. Three men from Hawkshead lost their lives in the Second World War, but as far as is known, none from Sawrey.

Notes

1. Taylor, Willow, *Through the Pages of Life and My Encounters with Beatrix Potter*, p. 53.
2. Lane, *The Magic Years of Beatrix Potter*, p. 159.
3. Brown, *Herdwicks: Herdwick Sheep and the English Lake District*, p. 87.
4. *The Times*, 7 August 1945.

CHAPTER 30

The Traditional View is Challenged

S O FAR IN this narrative the traditional and widely-held view of Beatrix has been questioned. That is that her parents', and in particular her mother's, over-protectiveness, coupled perhaps with a degree of possessiveness, and a desire to control, had condemned Beatrix to a cocooned life in which she was virtually isolated from her childhood peers. This had driven Beatrix, for self-preservation, to seek solace in her hobbies and in the writing of her journal.

Had this been the case, then one might naturally have expected that when Beatrix left home and escaped the clutches of her mother, her father having since died, she would have reverted to her natural self – enjoyed parties, entertained, and organized social gatherings – in other words had what may be described as 'fun'. However, this was not the case, as the following remarks by friends, acquaintances, and family members indicate. John Heelis said of Beatrix:

> She was tough and forbidding when she thought it necessary, and often seemed lost in her own thoughts, passing people by, head down, without a word.[1]

Mrs Rogerson, the housekeeper at Castle Cottage, 'found Beatrix very quiet and secretive at times. When she was engrossed in her writing she would hardly speak for days.'[2]

Lady Ulla Hyde Parker declared of Beatrix:

> She did not invite friendships. There were people whom she had known for years, and yet one could not say that real friendship existed between them and her. She was always kind but closed up ...[3]

Ulla said of Beatrix and her husband William, 'They were certainly a happy or, perhaps better, a contented couple ... But inside Cousin Beatie [as Ulla called her] there was a hidden world of her own.'[4]

Willow Taylor said of Beatrix that she

> always supported and encouraged the Guide movement. She allowed Guide companies from the cities to camp in Bull Banks in New Sawrey. [She herself would] occasionally ... come to the camp-fires but she always sat apart from the rest of us, for she never seemed comfortable in a group.[5] William Postlethwaite kept the farm called High Green Gate, opposite the Smithy [blacksmith] in Market Street. Beatrix Potter and William Postlethwaite were always arguing about something or other. William told Beatrix she ought to go and live on an island away from everybody.[6]

It may be concluded from these remarks that, rather than reverting to a more extroverted lifestyle, Beatrix, in her independent adult life, continued in a similar way to that which she had adopted previously. In other words, she was by nature an introvert.

* * *

Notes

1. Heelis, *The Tale of Mrs William Heelis: Beatrix Potter*, p. 7.
2. Ibid, p. 61.

3. Hyde Parker, *Cousin Beatie: a Memory of Beatrix Potter*, p. 19.
4. Ibid, p. 23.
5. Taylor, Willow, *Through the Pages of Life and My Encounters with Beatrix Potter*, p. 37.
6. Ibid, p. 33.

Epilogue

AVING established that Beatrix was an introvert, it is now possible to see her life in an entirely different light. Beatrix makes clear in her journal that, yes, there were times when she felt irritated and frustrated by her parents, Mrs Potter in particular. And she describes Bolton Gardens as her 'unloved birthplace', and declares, after it was destroyed by enemy bombing in 1940, 'I am rather pleased to hear it is no more.' Such remarks have been hitherto regarded as an indictment by Beatrix of her parents, for over-regimenting her life and isolating her from her peers. But was not the *real* reason why she disliked Bolton Gardens so much the fact that, in the polluted air of London, she suffered recurring colds and chest complaints? And also, that of course, she longed to live in the country rather than in the city?

Mr Potter's letters to Beatrix demonstrate clearly that he was a devoted father and, from Beatrix's journal, it is equally clear that Mrs Potter was most concerned for her daughter's welfare, whatever else her faults may have been. And rather than restricting Beatrix's life, some might say that they were excessively *indulgent* towards their daughter, for instance, by allowing her, and Bertram, to commandeer the nursery for a natural history

184

'museum' and artists' studio, and for allowing her to keep a large variety of pets, which she was permitted to take on holiday with her. Furthermore, Mr Potter encouraged Beatrix in her studies of natural history. He also took her to art exhibitions and encouraged her in her own artistic endeavours, by providing her with an art teacher and painting materials, and introducing her to Sir John Millais while other members of the family provided her with the reading material which gave her a good grounding in literature. These were hugely important factors in Beatrix's subsequent success as an author/illustrator. As for being deprived of the company of her peers, Beatrix seldom complained of this.

Lady Ulla Hyde Parker said of Beatrix, 'I sensed great warmth, but at the same time great reserve, even shyness.' But 'shyness' is perhaps the wrong word, for Beatrix could be extremely forthright, should the need arise. If she chose to withdraw from company or conversation, this was more likely to be on account of her introversion – whereby her mind could only be engaged by those who shared her interests – rather than 'shyness'. Ulla also refers to the 'loneliness she [Beatrix] had felt, from the disappointments and hurts life had inflicted on her'. This was true. Beatrix had experienced 'hurts', especially on account of her parents' attitude to her fiancé, Norman Warne, and his tragic and untimely death. But Beatrix was seldom 'lonely', and rarely, if ever, complained of being so.

Today Beatrix is remembered chiefly for her charming and entertaining tales of little animals from nature, attired in human clothes and speaking with human voices. Her stories are full of life, vigour, colour, and sheer *joie de vivre*. And millions of children throughout the world, and not a few adults, who also appreciate her work, should be grateful to her parents, Helen and Rupert Potter, for allowing Beatrix to be herself – an introvert – and retreat, when she chose to do so, into a private world of her own where she could be creative.

It is fitting to end this narrative, just as John Heelis did in his biography of Beatrix, by quoting what he describes as 'one of the last fragments of her writing. . .'.

BEATRIX POTTER

I will go back to the hills again
When the day's work is done
And set my hands against the rocks
Warm with an April sun
And see the night creep down the fells
And the stars climb one by one.[1]

Notes

1. Heelis, *The Tale of Mrs William Heelis: Beatrix Potter*, p. 156.

T HE SITE where Bolton Gardens once stood is now occupied by a school (only one of the five original pairs of semi-detached properties having survived to this day). Beatrix left the majority of her books and watercolour paintings to public libraries and art galleries. More than 300 of her paintings of fungi, together with her collection of mycological reference books, were donated, at her expressed wish, to the Armitt Trust Library, Ambleside; twenty-five of those which she created for Charles McIntosh were donated, after the death of William Heelis, to the Perth Museum and Art Gallery.

Beatrix stipulated that, in the event of her rooms at Hill Top being preserved in her memory, their contents were to be displayed in a particular way, and also that certain items of which she was particularly fond were to be transferred there from Castle Cottage.[1] This came to pass and, in 1946, the National Trust opened the property to the public. In 1951 the Lake District National Park was created.

The Potter tradition of Unitarianism was continued by Ronald Potter Jones MA FRIBA, a cousin of Beatrix born in Liverpool in 1876. Having graduated from Magdalen College, Oxford, he trained as an architect and became a Fellow of the Royal Institute of British Architects, one of his creations being the Unitarian

Church at Cambridge. In 1900 he left Liverpool for London and, in 1904, joined Essex Church in Kensington. A generous benefactor of the church, he donated a font, a carved pulpit, choir stalls, and marble tiling in the chancel. In 1908 he joined the Executive Committee of the British and Foreign Unitarian Association. Six years later his book *Nonconformist Church Architecture* was published by the Lindsey Press. He died on 2 October 1965 in his ninetieth year.[2]

Certain subsequent portrayals of Beatrix's life would undoubtedly have caused her to scowl with annoyance. However, one of which she most certainly would have approved was the Royal Ballet's production of 'The Tales of Beatrix Potter', created in 1971 by choreographer Sir Frederic Ashton, with music by John Lanchbery.

In 1973 Leslie Linder and his sister Enid left their large collection of Beatrix Potter memorabilia, including watercolour paintings, drawings, sketchbooks, other books, literary manuscripts, correspondence, and photographs, to the Victoria & Albert Museum ('The Linder Bequest'). Ten years later, Frederick Warne was acquired by Penguin Group (UK).

The Beatrix Potter Society was founded in 1980 to promote the study and appreciation of Beatrix's life in all its aspects; to protect the integrity of her unique works and bequests, and to promote her aims: 'The Society brings together on a worldwide basis those people who share these interests.'

The National Trust currently owns more than a quarter of the Lake District National Park, founded in 1951. The Herdwick Sheep Breeders' Association continues to flourish, this variety being the commonest to be seen on the hills of Lakeland.

The mission of the Royal Botanic Gardens, Kew, now, as then:

> is to ensure better management of the Earth's environment by increasing our knowledge and understanding of the plant kingdom: the basis of life on earth. Wherever possible, the Royal Botanic Gardens at Kew will endeavour to reduce and reverse the rate of destruction of the world's plant species and their habitats.

Surely Beatrix would have concurred completely with these sentiments.

Notes

1. Heelis, John, *The Tale of Mrs William Heelis: Beatrix Potter*, pp. 144–5.
2. *The Inquirer*, 16 October and 6 November 1965.

Beatrix's Unitarian Forebears

B EATRIX'S forebears, on both sides of the family, were Unitarians who believed not only in embracing the faith but also giving practical meaning to its tenets of humanity and compassion. Beatrix's paternal grandfather, calico manu-facturer Edmund Potter, for example, provided a reading room and library at his Dinting Vale works at Glossop in Derbyshire for the members of his workforce. He was also a principal contributor to the fund for creating the new Glossop (Unitarian) Chapel. When, in about 1840, he acquired Dinting Mill he converted its upper storey into a day school for the younger children of the mill's employees, and for the part-time workers at his print works. Of this enlightened employer it was said that each year he:

> presented book prizes for good work and good attendance ... He did not include religious education in the curriculum – he considered that school education should be purely secular and that religious education should be left to the churches. [Furthermore, in December 1873, he] ... built and furnished, at his own expense, a dining room for the

workers, in which 350 people were able to sit down to good warm meals provided at the cheapest possible rates.[1]

Beatrix's maternal grandmother, Jane Leech, of Gorse Hall Stalybridge, also took the opportunity to do good works. With the outbreak of the American Civil War in 1861, the year in which her husband, John (I), died, supplies of cotton from the USA dwindled alarmingly, with the result that the winter of 1862 'found 7,000 [cotton] operatives without employment in Stalybridge, and a vast number only partially employed'. This led to the so-called 'Bread Riots' of 1863. Jane responded by allowing part of her former residence, Hob Hill House, to be used as an institute where classes were provided for the benefit of the cotton workers and their wives and children. Jane's daughters, Elizabeth and Helen (Beatrix's mother), taught the womenfolk practical skills such as cookery, needlework and housecrafts and a kitchen also provided food for the hungry. Jane also permitted part of Hob Hill House to be used as premises for Stalybridge's first Unitarian Sunday School, which opened on 13 July 1862.

Originally the Unitarians of Stalybridge used the People's Hall in Corporation Street as their place of worship. When a new, purpose-built Stalybridge Unitarian Church was proposed, Jane's sons, John (II) and William Leech, donated a suitable site and they, together with Jane herself and Mr Potter (who six years earlier had married Jane's daughter, Helen), each donated the sum of £200. Jane laid the foundation stone on Whit Sunday 1869 and, to commemorate the occasion, presented a *Holy Bible* to the congregation. On 20 February the following year, the first service was conducted in the newly-opened church by the Reverend Gaskell. More than a decade later, on 18 May 1883, William Leech Esq. laid the foundation stone of Stalybridge's Unitarian School 'amidst great rejoicing'.[2]

Beatrix's parents also followed the Unitarian tradition. As a student in Manchester Mr Potter worshipped at the city's Upper Brook Street (Unitarian) Chapel where his tutor, the Reverend Dr John James Tayler (Principal of Manchester New College from 1853–69) was minister, and at Hyde (Unitarian) Chapel,

Gee Cross, Hyde, Cheshire. (Hyde was Mr Potter's wife-to-be, Helen's, home town, and Rupert and Helen were married on 8 August 1863 at Hyde Chapel, where her parents worshipped, by its minister, the Reverend Charles Beard.)

Unitarianism originated in Transylvania, now part of Romania, in the sixteenth century. Its ideas were first expounded in England by John Biddle (1615–62), graduate and tutor of Magdalen Hall, Oxford, and, in 1774, Britain's first Unitarian congregation was established by former Anglican clergyman Theophilus Lindsey in Essex Street, Strand, London.

To Unitarians Jesus Christ is not God (i.e. part of the Trinity), but rather 'a man, unequivocally human [who was] conceived and born in the usual human manner'.[3] God is therefore regarded by Unitarians as a 'unity', rather than a 'trinity' – hence the name 'Unitarian'. Unitarians also believe that following Christ's crucifixion, he did not descend into 'Hell' for in Unitarianism there is no such place. Neither is there such an entity as 'The Devil' and neither do they subscribe to the doctrine of Original Sin. The Resurrection of Christ from the dead is to be seen not as a literal truth, but rather as a 'powerful myth';[4] and as for the notion of there being life after death, 'most Unitarians agree that this is an area of mystery'.[5]

Notes

1. Godfrey, *A Genial Man: Edmund Potter and his Calico Printing Work*. Beatrix Potter Studies, XI.
2. Hill, *Bygone Stalybridge*, p. 123.
3. Reed, *Unitarian? What's that?* Para. 12.
4. Reed, *Beatrix Potter's Unitarian Context*, p. 5.
5. Ibid, p. 9

Appendix 3

Sir John Millais

BORN IN Southampton in 1829, Millais was brought up mainly in the Channel Islands. In December 1840, at the age of eleven, he became the youngest student ever admitted to the Royal Academy Schools. He made his first visit to Scotland in late June 1853, discovering the ideal country in which to fish, shoot and paint. There, however, he specialized in landscapes, rather than in the commissioned portraits which he was accustomed to paint when at home in London.

In July 1855 Millais married Euphemia – 'Effie' (née Gray, former wife of author and art critic John Ruskin) – whose family home was Bowerwell House, Perth. The marriage took place in somewhat scandalous circumstances and the couple therefore thought it prudent to remain in Scotland for a while until, in 1861, they relocated to London, and 7 Cromwell Place, South Kensington. Millais' love for Scotland was deep and abiding and he returned there almost every year to spend several months fishing, shooting, or deerstalking. Favourite locations were St Mary's Tower and, subsequently, Birnam Hall, both beside the River Tay at Little Dunkeld in Perthshire. He was elected to the Royal Academy in 1863.

Millais was in the habit of asking Mr Potter to take photographs of the subjects which he was painting at the time. They included various people, including children, landscapes and an apple tree. 'Mr Millais says the professionals [photographers] aren't fit to hold a candle to papa,' said Beatrix.[1]

In 1877 Millais painted portraits based on two characters from the novels of Sir Walter Scott, 'The Bride of Lammermoor' (from the novel of the same name) and 'Effie Deans' (from *The Heart of Midlothian*). The model for the latter portrait was none other than twenty-four-year-old Lillie Langtry, the new mistress of Edward, the Prince of Wales, who like Millais, originated from the Channel Islands.[2] A photograph exists of Lillie and Mr Potter together and it is highly likely that he photographed her for Millais who also painted Lillie and called the work 'The Jersey Lily'. In that same year Millais and Effie moved from Cromwell Place to No. 2 Palace Gate, a splendid mansion (also in the district of Kensington) which Millais had built for himself.

Notes
1. Ibid, 10 January 1884.
2. Millais, *The Life and Letters of Sir John Everett Millais*, pp. 256–7.

APPENDIX 4

Sir Henry Roscoe

B ORN IN London in 1833 Roscoe attended Liverpool Institute for Boys and University College, London, before travelling to Heidelberg to study under German chemist and physicist Robert Wilhelm Bunsen. In 1853 he was elected Fellow of the Royal Society; from 1857 to 1885 he was Professor of Chemistry at Owens College, Manchester; in 1873 he was awarded the Royal Society's Royal Medal; in 1884 he was knighted 'in acknowledgement of his distinguished service on the Technical Education Commission'; in 1885 he became Member of Parliament for South Manchester, and in 1909 was appointed privy councillor. He was also passionately interested in education, being the author of several textbooks on chemistry.

In Beatrix's time the Royal Botanic Gardens, Kew, in south-west London, housed the largest and finest collection of plants in the world. The gardens were not simply for the benefit of tourists, for this was the botanical nerve centre of the British Empire where decisions were made that would affect the lives of millions.

Although, in the nineteenth century, Kew was an almost entirely male preserve, the gardens owed their existence to Augusta, Dowager Princess of Wales and mother of King George III, in whose royal estate it lay originally. It was Augusta who, in 1759, had laid out three-and-a-half hectares of her estate as a botanic garden, employing William Aiton as head gardener, John Stuart, 3rd Earl of Bute, as her botanical advisor and Sir William Chambers as her architect. Chambers' creations included the Orangery and the Pagoda. The Palm House, constructed between 1844 and 1848, was designed by another architect, Decimus Burton.

On Augusta's death in 1772, George III (1738–1820) enlarged Kew by adding to it the adjacent Richmond Estate of his late grandfather, George I. He encouraged and supported Sir Joseph Bankes, Kew's unofficial director, to develop the gardens, and at Bankes' instigation collectors were despatched to scour the world for plants of 'economic, scientific or horticultural interest'.[1]

George III's wife, Queen Charlotte, was also a botanical enthusiast (who housed her botanical collections and library of botanical books in a cottage in the grounds of Windsor Castle). She arranged for her daughters to be given lessons in flower painting by Margaret Meen (1775–1824) from Bungay in Suffolk (founder and illustrator of the periodical *Exotic Plants from the Royal Gardens at Kew*, 1790, of which only two issues were published), and also by Austrian microscopist and botanical artist, Francis (Franz Andreas) Bauer. The royals were given 'regular lectures in zoology and botany' by Sir James Edward Smith, founder of the Linnean Society of London and its first president.[2]

In 1840 Kew was adopted as a national botanic garden with Sir William Jackson Hooker, Professor of Botany at Glasgow University, as its Director. Hooker established Kew's Museums, its Department of Economic Botany, its Herbarium (repository of preserved plant specimens), and its Library. In 1865 he was succeeded by his son, Sir Joseph Dalton Hooker, under whose aegis the Jodrell Research Laboratory was opened (1876). When the latter retired in 1885 he was succeeded by William T. Thiselton-Dyer, husband of his eldest daughter, Harriet (a skilled artist and contributor of drawings to the *Botanical Magazine*).

Roscoe did more than merely give Beatrix a 'note'. He promised, personally, to accompany her to Kew and introduce her to its director. (It is interesting that, almost a century earlier, Roscoe's paternal grandfather, William, had been a benefactor of Liverpool's Roylean Herbarium, bequeathed to Liverpool Royal Institution by John Forbes Royle, Director of the Saharanpur Botanic Garden, Uttar Pradesh, India, and, between 1806 and 1817, had contributed 5,000 or so plants to that establishment.)

On Wednesday 20 May 1896 Beatrix and her uncle duly set out, by train, for Kew where they first met Daniel Morris (later Sir), one of Kew's assistant directors who 'disclaimed all knowledge of fungi', saying that he (i.e. his speciality) was 'exclusively tropical'. This was perfectly true: Morris's expertise lay in the relevance of plants to the agricultural economy of the Caribbean. Of William B. Hemsley, a principal assistant, and of John G. Baker, Keeper of the Kew Herbarium, Beatrix said little. However, she found George Massee, Principal Assistant at the Herbarium 'a very pleasant, kind gentleman who seemed to like my drawings'.[3]

Notes
1. Bromley, G. and M. Maunder, *Royal Botanic Gardens, Kew.* pp. 4–5.
2. Desmond, Ray, *The History of the Royal Botanic Gardens, Kew*, p. 79.
3. Linder, op. cit., 19 May 1896.

The Advancement of
Women

EVEN BEFORE Beatrix was born, enlightened people of both sexes were striving to improve the lives of women, in particular through the Women's Movement (which began in Britain in 1872 with the foundation of the National Society for Women's Suffrage) which was dedicated to establishing the social, political, and economic equality of women with men. In the vanguard of the movement were Unitarians, both women and men.

Harriet Martineau (born 1802), sister of Dr James Martineau, was taught mainly at home but also, from 1813 to 1815, at the Reverend Isaac Perry's Unitarian school for both boys and girls in Norwich. She subsequently went to Bristol to a boarding school run by her aunt, Mrs Kentish. She became a journalist and a writer, vehicles she used to express her views on women's rights. She was also a political economist and an abolitionist and argued that 'Every human being [i.e. both male and female] is to be made as perfect as possible [and] this must be done through the most comprehensive development of all the faculties'.[1]

Harriet's siblings were also firm believers in education. Her sister Rachel founded a school for girls at Liverpool where a 'thorough intellectual education' was provided and where her brother James taught Latin, mathematics, history, botany and the New Testament.[2] James also gave 'University Extension' lectures (for those who were not full-time students) for women in Manchester.

Elizabeth Gaskell (born 1810), wife of the Reverend William Gaskell, was educated first at home, then from the age of eleven at a boarding school for girls at Barford, Warwickshire, run by the three Byerley sisters (who were Anglicans, but accepted Unitarian pupils). Three years later she transferred to Avonbank, another boarding school at nearby Stratford-on-Avon. The heroines in Elizabeth's novels 'strongly reflect the determination and trials of contemporary women'.[3] However, she herself recognized, as the wife of a minister of religion, how difficult it was for a woman to be artistically creative on the one hand, and homely and domestic on the other. She articulateds this dilemma in her *Life of Charlotte Brontë*, where she contrasted the life of Charlotte Brontë, the author, with that of Charlotte the woman: 'There were separate duties belonging to each character, not impossible, but difficult to be reconciled.'[4]

A strong, male advocate of women's rights was John Relly Beard, Unitarian Minister of Greengate Chapel, Salford, Lancashire, educational reformer, and Principal of Manchester College from 1854 to 1874, whose son, the Reverend Charles, had officiated at Mr and Mrs Potter's wedding. Beard firmly believed that girls should experience 'the highest university learning no less than boys'[5] and supported the Working Women's College, Fitzroy Street, London, founded in 1864, which aimed 'by systematic teaching given in evening classes, to supply to women occupied during the day, a higher education than is generally within their reach'.[6] He also declared that men and women alike required 'a common educational discipline'[7] and that 'to educate a mother is to educate a family, and the education of families is the education of the race.'[8] But he was opposed to employing women in the mills and, in particular, the 'mothers of families'.[9]

Had it been Beatrix's wish, and that of her parents, that she attend school, then opportunities to do so were available for girls, even in the 1870s. Frances Buss, wife of a painter and etcher, had founded a private school for young boys and girls in London's Kentish Town in 1845, and in the same premises her daughter, Frances Mary Buss, founded a morning school offering young ladies a liberal education. In 1850 the schools combined in a larger building which became the North London Collegiate School for Ladies (NLC) with Frances Mary Buss as headmistress. The fees were £2. 2s per pupil per quarter. In 1870 the 'Buss School' was placed in the hands of trustees and Frances Mary founded the Camden School for Girls, which offered a more affordable education.

Should Beatrix have wished to go on from school to university, then this too would have been possible, for a great breakthrough had come in 1878 when London University became the first in Britain to admit women as full-time degree students. At University College, one of London University's constituent colleges, a department for Beatrix's favourite subject, botany, was established in its own right and, in 1881, Alice Mitchell and Mary Isabella Webb, both of London University's Bedford College, became the first students to be awarded degrees in botany (both B.Sc. Second Class, with Honours).[10] In1909 botanist, mycologist, and pioneer suffragette Helen Gwynne-Vaughan (1879–1967, née Fraser), born into a family of Scottish aristocrats, became Professor of Botany at London University's Birkbeck College. Eight decades earlier, in 1829, John Lindley, University College London's first Professor of Botany (1829–1860), drew the distinction between botany as an 'amusement for ladies', and botanical science as 'an occupation for the serious thoughts of man'.[11] His remark now seemed but a distant memory.

Should Beatrix have wished to apply for membership of the British Mycological Society (founded in 1896), that too would have been possible for the society had admitted women almost from its inception. As regards the Linnean Society, it was through the untiring efforts of botany enthusiast Mrs Marian Sarah Ogilvie Farquharson (1846–1912), that, on 17 November 1904, women – sixteen in all – were first admitted as members. (Farquharson was an expert on the higher cryptogams, plants with no flowers or seeds, such as ferns, mosses, algae, and fungi, and author of *A Pocket Guide to British Ferns*, published in 1881. She did not possess a university degree, having received her education at home.) Of these sixteen women perhaps the most notable was Annie Lorrain Smith (1892–1937) who studied seaweeds, fungi, and lichens at the British Museum (Natural History), was President of the British Mycological Society in 1907 and, in 1917, wrote the standard *Handbook of British Lichens*.

Despite these advances, it was many years before higher education for women, even wealthy ones from middle or upper class families, was considered the norm. The above remarks, however, as far as Beatrix was concerned, were of purely theoretical interest. She had no desire to attend school. Even if she had, Mrs Potter would probably have forbidden it for fear of her catching 'germs'.

As for the Women's Movement, so consumed was Beatrix by her hobbies that it entirely passed her by. And as for the suffragettes, she described their work as being 'very silly',[12] which implies that she was quite content for men to continue in their traditional role.

Notes
1. Martineau, Harriet, *Household Education*, pp. 221–6.
2. Watts, *Gender, Power and the Unitarians in England 1760–1860*, p. 135–6.
3. Matthew, H.C.G., and Brian Harrison, *Oxford Dictionary of National Biography*.
4. Gaskell, *The Life of Charlotte Brontë*, Pt 2, Chapter 2.
5. Watts, op. cit., p. 156.
6. *Woman's Mission*, p. 434.
7. Watts, Ruth, op. cit., p. 191.
8. Ibid, p. 194.
9. Ibid, p. 174.
10. Archives, Royal Holloway, University of London.
11. Lindley, John. Inaugural Lecture as Professor of Botany at the University of London, 1829. Quoted in Shteir, Ann B. 1996. *Cultivating Women, Cultivating Science: Flora's Daughters and Botany in England, 1760–1780*. p. 157.
12. Lane, *The Tale of Beatrix Potter*, p. 106.

APPENDIX 6

Possible Causes for Bertram's Stroke

I S IT POSSIBLE that excessive drinking could have been the
cause of Bertram's stroke? The answer is yes, and for several
reasons. It is now known that excessive alcohol intake can
cause or exacerbate high blood pressure, irregularities of the
heartbeat, known as atrial fibrillation, or damage to the heart
muscle with consequent deterioration of its function, known as
cardiomyopathy, all of which can, in turn, predispose to stroke.
Significantly, in respect of Bertram's stroke, excessive alcohol
intake can also inhibit the coagulation of blood, which pre-
disposes to haemorrhaging from the blood vessels, including
those supplying the brain.[14]

The question arises: was it Bertram's alcoholic tendencies
which prompted Beatrix to declare, in June 1884, that 'the best
upbringing has sometimes failed in this family, and I am afraid
that Bertram has *it* in him'? By 'in this family', did she also have
in mind her uncle, William Leech, of whom she wrote on 8 March
1887, after his death, 'He had an inflammation of the lungs with
which he had no chance owing to the horrible condition of his
body through drink?'[15] And could the fact that Bertram drank
also explain why he was 'taken ill with pleurisy' at Charterhouse

School in April 1887, and why Beatrix followed this up with the strange comment, 'of which it is useless to speak more, for the thing is done and can never be undone'.[16] Could Bertram's chest pain have been due not to 'pleurisy', but to excessive consumption of alcohol (for which misdemeanour at least one boy was expelled from the school in the late nineteenth century), which may adversely affect the heart 'by making it beat faster and harder. The alcohol may even produce irregular and in-effective heart beats. The increased need of such a heart for oxygen may be sufficient to produce chest pain. Cessation of the alcohol is all that is needed to eliminate the chest pain.'[1]

Finally, heavy cigarette smoking cannot be ruled out, both as a possible cause of Bertram's pleurisy, if that is indeed what it was, and also as a cause of his cerebral haemorrhage, cigarettes being known to cause damage to the lining of the arteries.

Note
1. *Drinking and Stroke Risk*, January 2007, University of South Carolina, USA.

Appendix 7

The Reverend
Hardwicke Rawnsley

ORN IN 1851, Rawnsley, the son of the Vicar of Shiplake-on-Thames Parish Church, Oxfordshire, was educated at Uppingham School where Edward Thring was his headmaster and also his godfather. Thring had a holiday home at Grasmere in the heart of Lakeland, to which he used to invite Rawnsley for the summer holidays. There he instilled in the youth a love for the Lake District and for the so-called Lake poets, William Wordsworth, a native of the area, and Samuel Taylor Coleridge and Robert Southey who came to live there.

Having graduated in natural science, with chemistry as his special subject, from Balliol College, Oxford, Rawnsley worked for a time in Soho in London's West End and in Clifton, Bristol. In 1875 he was ordained deacon and, in 1877, priest. The following year he became Vicar of St Margaret's Church, Wray and married Edith Fletcher of Croft, Ambleside, who bore him a son, Noel.

Bibliography

Battrick, Elizabeth, *The Real World of Beatrix Potter* (Jarrold & Sons, Norwich, for the National Trust, 1987, first published in 1983)

Beatrix Potter Studies III, *Beatrix Potter before Peter Rabbit* (The Beatrix Potter Society, London, 1988)

Beatrix Potter Studies XI, *Beatrix Potter's Family and Friends* (The Beatrix Potter Society, London, 2004)

Beatrix Potter Studies XII, *Beatrix Potter: Sources of Her Inspiration* (The Beatrix Potter Society, London, 2006)

Binnie, G. A. C., *The Churches and Graveyards of Roxburghshire* (2001)

Britten, James (editor), *Journal of Botany* (Taylor & Francis, London, 1922)

Bromley, G., and M. Maunder, *Royal Botanic Gardens, Kew* (HMSO, London, 1994)

Brown, Geoff, *Herdwicks: Herdwick Sheep and the English Lake District* (Hayloft Publishing, Kirkby Stephen, Cumbria, 2009)

Bulletin of Miscellaneous Information: Royal Botanic Gardens, Kew.

Caldecott, Randolph, *A Frog He Would A-Wooing Go* (F. Warne, London, 1883)

Coates, Henry, *A Perthshire Naturalist* (T. Fisher Unwin, London, 1923)

Collins, Vere H., *Talks with Thomas Hardy at Max Gate* (Duckworth, London, 1978)

Coppins, B. J. (editor), *Notes from the Royal Botanic Garden Edinburgh* 44(3). Article by Mary Noble, *Beatrix Potter, Naturalist & Mycologist and Charles McIntosh, the 'Perthshire Naturalist'* (HMSO, Edinburgh, 1987)

Cowell, F. R., *The Athenaeum* (Heinemann Educational Books, London, 1975)

Crane, Walter, *The Baby's Opera* (Frederick Warne, London, 1877)

Denyer, Susan, *Beatrix Potter and her Farms* (The National Trust, Swindon, 1992)

Denyer, Susan, *Beatrix Potter: At Home in the Lake District* (Frances Lincoln, London, 2004)

Desmond, Ray, *The History of the Royal Botanic Gardens, Kew* (The Harvil Press, London, 1998)

Gage, Andrew T., and William T. Stern, *Bicentenary History of the Linnean Society of London* (Academic Press, London, 1988)

Gaskell, Elizabeth C., *The Life of Charlotte Brontë* (Smith, Elder, London, 1857)

Gatford, Hazel, *Beatrix Potter: Her Art and Inspiration* (The National Trust, Swindon, 2004)

Griffiths, Major Arthur, *Clubs and Clubmen* (Hutchinson, London, 1907)

Harvie-Brown, J. A., James W. H. Trail and William Eagle Clarke (editors), *The Annals of Scottish Natural History* (David Douglas, Edinburgh, January 1904)

Heelis, John, *The Tale of Mrs William Heelis: Beatrix Potter* (Sutton Publishing, Stroud, 2003)

Helgoe, Laurie, *Introvert Power: Why Your Inner Life is your Hidden Strength* (Sourcebooks, Naperville, Illinois, 2008)

Hill, Samuel, *Bygone Stalybridge* (M. T. D. Rigg Publications, Leeds, Yorkshire, 1907)

Hollindale, Peter, *Aesop in the Shadows* (The Beatrix Potter Society, London, 1997)

Hyde Parker, Ulla, *Cousin Beatie: a Memory of Beatrix Potter* (Frederick Warne, London, 1981)

Joy, Libby, and Judy Taylor (editors), *Beatrix Potter's Family and Friends. Beatrix Potter Studies XI* (The Beatrix Potter Society, London, 2005)

Joy, Libby (producer), *Beatrix Potter: Sources of her Inspiration. Beatrix Potter Studies XII* (The Beatrix Potter Society, London, 2006)

Lane, Margaret, *The Magic Years of Beatrix Potter* (Frederick Warne, London, 1978)

Lane, Margaret, *The Tale of Beatrix Potter* (Penguin Books, London, 2001)

Lear, Linda, *Beatrix Potter: A Life in Nature* (St Martin's Press, New York, 2007)

Linder, Leslie, *A History of the Writings of Beatrix Potter* (Frederick Warne, London, 1971)

Linder, Leslie (editor), *The Journal of Beatrix Potter from 1881–1897* (Frederick Warne, London, 1966)

206

Lockhart, J. G., *The Life of Sir Walter Scott* (abridgement) (T. & A. Constable, Edinburgh, 1972)

Maloney, Margaret Crawford (editor), *Dear Ivy, Dear June: Letters from Beatrix Potter* (Friends of the Osborne and Lillian H. Smith Collections, Toronto, 1977)

Martineau, James, *Common Prayer for Christian Worship* (Walker Wise, Boston, USA, 1863)

Martineau, Harriet, *Household Education* (E. Moxon, London, 1848)

Matthew, H. C. G., and Brian Harrison (editors), *Oxford Dictionary of National Biography* (Oxford University Press, Oxford, 2004)

Millais, John Guille, *The Life and Letters of Sir John Everett Millais* (Methuen, London, 1905)

Morse, Jane Crowell (editor), *Beatrix Potter's Americans: Selected Letters* (The Horn Book, Inc, Boston, USA, 1982)

Nelson, Claudia, *Family Ties in Victorian England* (Praeger Publishers, Westport, CT, 2007)

Noble, Mary, *Beatrix Potter and her Funguses*. Beatrix Potter Studies I. 41–6. Paper given at Ambleside to the Beatrix Potter Society (1984)

Potter, Beatrix, *The Fairy Caravan* (Penguin Books, London, 1992)

Proceedings of the Linnean Society of London from November 1896 to June 1897 (Linnean Society, London)

Purvis, June, *A History of Women's Education in England* (Open University Press, Buckingham, UK, 1991)

Rawnsley, Eleanor F., *Canon Rawnsley: An Account of his Life* (Maclehose, Jackson, Glasgow, 1923)

Rawnsley, the Reverend Hardwicke, *By Fell and Dale in the English Lakes* (James Maclehose & Sons, Glasgow, 1911)

Reed, the Reverend Clifford M., *Beatrix Potter's Unitarian Context*. Published in, *Beatrix Potter: Thirty Years of Discovery and Appreciation*, Joy & Judy Taylor (editors) (Beatrix Potter Society, 2010)

Reed, the Reverend Clifford M., *Unitarian? What's that?* (Lindsey Press, London, 1999)

Roscoe, Sir Henry Enfield, *The Life & Experiences of Sir Henry Enfield Roscoe* (Macmillan, London, 1906)

Roscoe, Sir Henry Enfield, Obituary notices of Fellows deceased (The Royal Society, London)

Ruston, Alan, *Unitarianism: The Continuing Story* (The General Assembly of Unitarian and Free Christian Churches, Essex Hall, London)

Slater's Royal National Commercial Directory of Lancashire, 1871–2, Part I (Isaac Slater, Manchester)

Scott, Sir Walter, *Rob Roy* (Macmillan, London, 1926)

Shteir, Ann B., *Cultivating Women, Cultivating Science: Flora's Daughters and Botany in England*, 1760–80 (Johns Hopkins University Press, Baltimore, 1996)

Smith, Leonard (editor), *The Athenaeum: Club and Social Life in London 1824–1974* (Heinemann, London, 1975)

Soames, Catherine, and Angus Stevenson (editors), *Oxford Dictionary of English* (Oxford University Press, Oxford, 2006)

Taylor, Judy (editor and writer), *Beatrix Potter: A Holiday Diary* (The Beatrix Potter Society, London, 1966)

Taylor, Judy, *Beatrix Potter: Artist, Storyteller and Countrywoman* (Frederick Warne, London, 2002)

Taylor, Judy, *Beatrix Potter and Hill Top* (The National Trust, Swindon, 1989)

Taylor, Judy, *Letters to Children from Beatrix Potter* (The Penguin Group, London, 1992)

Taylor, Judy (editor), *The Choyce Letters* (The Beatrix Potter Society, London, 1994)

Taylor, Judy, *Beatrix Potter: A Holiday Diary* (The Beatrix Potter Society, London, 1996)

Taylor, Judy, (editor), *Beatrix Potter's Farming Friendship: Lake District letters to Joseph Moscrop 1926–1943* (The Beatrix Potter Society, London, 1998)

Taylor, Judy, (selector and introducer), *Beatrix Potter's Letters* (Frederick Warne, London, 1989)

Taylor, Judy, Joyce Irene Whalley, Anne Stevenson Hobbs, and Elizabeth M. Battrick, *Beatrix Potter: The Artist and Her World* (The Penguin Books Group, London, 1987)

Taylor, M. A., and R. H. Rodger, *A Fascinating Acquaintance: Charles McIntosh & Beatrix Potter, their Common Bond in the Natural History of the Dunkeld area* (Perth Museum & Art Gallery, Perth, 2003)

Taylor, Willow, *Through the Pages of Life and My Encounters with Beatrix Potter* (The Beatrix Potter Society, London, 2005)

Turrill, William Bertram, *The Royal Botanic Gardens, Kew, Past and Present* (Herbert Jenkins, London, 1959)

Watts, Ruth, *Gender, Power and the Unitarians in England 1760–1860* (Longman, London and New York, 1998)

Wetherell, Elizabeth, *The Wide Wide World.* (Humphrey Milford, Oxford University Press, London, 1850)

Williams, Val, *Women Photographers* (Virago Press, London, 1986)